D1552594

No Ordinary Work

No Ordinary Work

Church Planting in the Shadow
of the Church Growth Movement

Larry Snyder

RESOURCE *Publications* · Eugene, Oregon

NO ORDINARY WORK
Church Planting in the Shadow of the Church Growth Movement

Copyright © 2021 Larry Snyder. All rights reserved. Except for brief quotations in critical publications or reviews, no part of this book may be reproduced in any manner without prior written permission from the publisher. Write: Permissions, Wipf and Stock Publishers, 199 W. 8th Ave., Suite 3, Eugene, OR 97401.

Resource Publications
An Imprint of Wipf and Stock Publishers
199 W. 8th Ave., Suite 3
Eugene, OR 97401

www.wipfandstock.com

PAPERBACK ISBN: 978-1-6667-0033-6
HARDCOVER ISBN: 978-1-6667-0034-3
EBOOK ISBN: 978-1-6667-0035-0

Manufactured in the U.S.A.   JUNE 11, 2021

Scripture quotations are from the ESV® Bible (The Holy Bible, English Standard Version®), copyright © 2001 by Crossway, a publishing ministry of Good News Publishers. Used by permission. All rights reserved.

This book is dedicated to Mindy, my bride and greatest partner in ministry. You always believe in me, you cheer me on, and you still reach for my hand when walking by my side. To Jesus, my Savior and always the best church planter. To church planters everywhere, I see you and I know your toil.

Contents

Acknowledgements

THANK YOU TO MY wife and children who have endured and labored with me during two church plants, many adventures, and limitless times of frustration. Thank you to the many partners over the years who have consisted of friends, family, churches, and the North American Mission Board. Your patient partnership through years of planting churches is still inconceivable to me. Thank you to Dr. Barry Whitworth and Dr. Mike Landry who have poured their lives into me over the years and helped me to live a life for Jesus that I never dreamed possible. Thank you to my biological parents now with the Lord, and my parents-in-love for supporting me in all my crazy adventures. Finally, thank you to Jesus for saving me and using me.

Introduction

EVERYONE TAKES THEIR AUTOMOBILE to the mechanic at some point and time. In our home, we rarely drive brand new cars because my wife is keenly aware of the loss of value once you drive them off the lot. So, we end up at the mechanic from time to time on top of our regular maintenance schedule. With that said, I always tend to seek out a "mom and pop" mechanic who is a Christian or at least works with a great level of integrity. I need a mechanic who is going to be able to go home and feel content because he did right by me and took good care of my car. The honest mechanic is required because I claim to do a lot of handyman stuff on my own, but rarely will I touch a car. Actually, if I am being completely honest, a mechanic could make up all kinds of names when telling me about the repairs that I need and I would probably just nod along and pretend that I have a clue. I can hear it now, "Mr. Snyder, your wizzlewop appears to be leaking something. It is starting to damage your fragnug and without a fragnug you might end up on the side of the road. We can replace it for $900." I blindly nod along and mumble, "Uh huh."

Why do you go to your mechanic? What is it that causes you to gravitate to their business? Is it because they have the most cars in the garage? Perhaps it is the plushness of their waiting room or the coffee they serve while you get your oil changed? Maybe the neon sign that hangs above their garage is the brightest and biggest? I doubt it. I'm guessing that, like most people, you take your car to a mechanic for reasons similar to me. Reasons that resemble integrity, fairness, hard work, a positive reputation, and a job well done.

With so many church planters seeking to be successful, many of the ways we measure success rarely share the same metrics we would ascribe to a successful mechanic. The measures of success that we adopt can often lead to personal disappointment, frustration, comparisons and even depression.

This can lead to planters who quit and churches that close even before they really got started, potentially ruining a witness to an entire community. What if the biblical metrics for church planting could be redefined and clarified in a way that replaces frustration with fire, and replaces disappointment with direction? What if the comparisons to steroid growth could be stopped and replaced with a better understanding of kingdom growth? In this book we will highlight each extraordinary aspect of church planting and detail the biblical metrics that can infuse in each church planter a better understanding of their own success and that of their new church start.

Over the course of the previous sixteen years, I have been blessed (and a little shell-shocked) to be able to plant two churches. My first church planting experience led me to south central Pennsylvania in 2006. The work was fueled by a healthy balance of wild idealism, bold initiative, crazy stupidity, a love for making disciples, a love for my home community, and a lot of naivete. I pastored that church for eleven years and found great joy in watching it grow, forming a family, and honoring Christ while never seeing it break 130 in Sunday attendance. At the end of those eleven years Jesus has led me to plant a second church in southwest Florida, but this time with a bit more of a reflective and honest spirit.

I have lived a life of extreme joys, undergirded by times of frustration, self-loathing and feelings of abject failure because my church, on the surface, rarely looked like other existing churches that surrounded me. And to boot, my church plant pretty much never looked like those being held up as examples at the many conferences and conventions that I would attend. I remember attending a conference for church planters in Atlanta about four years after arriving in Pennsylvania. I sat down on the first night in a large church auditorium and listened to a man who launched a church with over one hundred on his launch-team, share about the struggles of the early years of his own plant. His wife later shared how she made her husband promise that if the plant lasted longer than a year, he would hire a children's pastor for the staff so she didn't have to lead a children's ministry forever. Meanwhile, I launched with about twenty people and in year four, my wife was still faithfully serving as the children's ministry leader with no end in sight and certainly no staff on the horizon. I now saw myself not only as a horrible planter, but I was also a horrible husband. In that moment, I sat there wondering if this was the best use of $250.

Throughout my years as a church planter, I have found myself constantly being driven crazy by who I wasn't, what I wasn't doing and how fast I wasn't doing something. I do not claim to be an expert in church plant methodology. I've never served as senior pastor of a church larger than about 125 in attendance on any given Sunday. But I do know what it is like to minister under the weight of heavy expectations and constant comparisons.

Over the course of my ministry years as a church planter, I have been able to see first-hand the emotional and spiritual challenges that other church planters have carried, and in most cases I have been able to affirm my friends by saying, "I carry it, too." The fact of the matter is, that for reasons of spiritual, emotional and physical health, each planter needs to be able to recognize these challenges and categorize them as either rational, biblical challenges or man-made, irrational ones.

I would suspect that there might be someone picking up this book and they are about to venture into church planting for the first time. I've been you. I know what it is like to feel such a love for your new community and to have the courage to storm the gates of hell with a water pistol. You have your annual progressions all planned out, your vision and mission statement is spot on, and your partners are on board and ready to go with you. How will you respond when your facility location falls through? How will you respond when your first partner cuts funding a year earlier than expected? What do you lean on when the plans of man crumble? I pray that you find both hope and renewed purpose in this book.

There may be some existing church planters reading this book who have recently come to the realization that your church numbers look a lot different than what you were anticipating. You were planning on 300 in attendance each Sunday by year three. Yet you are sitting at forty-five in year two and you're worried that it is going to take longer than the three-year commitment that your partners and sending agency each made with you. Does your slower level of growth mean that you have failed? Does it mean that you should begin to put a plan in place to wind down your church planting endeavor? I pray that you find encouragement in this book to keep on going and that you find personal fulfillment in your calling.

There may even be some church planters reading this book who have taken a beating and in your abused condition, the whispers of the Evil One are eating your lunch and ruining your day, week, and year. Someone on your core team who seemed like the perfect fit is now sabotaging the vision that God gave you for reaching your community. As a result, you are starting to doubt yourself and even worse, you are starting to doubt God. Your family is stressed, and you are convinced that you are the worst father in the world.

I have been to each one of these places and on any given day, I'm still there. I can't tell you how many times I have required long walks and even longer conversations with God to keep from quitting. God has even used my wife on a lot of those long walks to talk some sense into me. Loneliness in the midst of doubt and depression is never a good place to be.

Allow me to transition with a question. If you knew that because of your faithful efforts, in twenty years your community would have a solid disciple-making church that wasn't there before, averaging between eighty and one hundred in weekly attendance, would you take God up on that opportunity? Even more, what if you knew the culture was changing so fast that in twenty years, we'd be living in a post-Christian American culture where the days of megachurches on seventy-five acres of land were an anomaly, would you count your church as a success?

As you read this book, you may not find each word appealing or helpful. You may not even agree with everything that is shared. That's okay. I understand because I read a lot of books and feel the same way. I just pray that as a church planter, something triggers in you that allows you to stop feeling like you need to be someone else or something else. The 1990s and early 2000s gave us the church growth movement. Out of that movement came some pretty incredible things such as innovative approaches to evangelism, creative thinking in light of our outreach programs and worship services. It also allowed for opportunities of increased influence in the cultural realm simply based upon size and money. One of the down sides of the church growth movement (especially during this increasingly anti-Christian environment in the western world) is the expectations of many who are in the Christian world, especially those in our pulpits, our seminaries and our agencies. Planting in the shadow of the church growth movement has created many unnecessary expectations and definitions of success that quite honestly, are not rooted in biblical metrics. I pray that in this lighthearted yet honest look at church planting, you find the peace in your heart and joy in your journey that sadly, so many planters seem to be missing out on today.

Metrics – The Necessary Evil

"So How Are You Doing?"

ONE OF THE GREAT guarantees of church planting has nothing to do with your church family or your accomplishments. It is the questioning that you will receive from those outside your church plant regarding what kind of "success" you are experiencing. They may not know you at all and simply feel they are being polite. They may love you and have life-long relationships with your family and in-turn ask questions about your progress as a church plant because their concern is genuine.

I have found that the most common question from those outside of my church plant towards me is usually, "So how are you all doing?" It is such a simple question to others and yet it can throw me into such a nauseating tailspin that I'm looking for the eject handle on a previously delightful conversation. The sister question is equally intimidating: "So how many are you all running?" One minute you're swapping stories about your respective children and the next minute you're scouring your brain for any relatable, significant thing that has happened in your church plant.

Your brain thrashes with potential responses. There was that family that came to small group and never came back because they're allergic to your cat. What about the guy who came with all the ideas on how to make your worship program look just like his last church? Or you might try the man who walked out halfway through your sermon causing all thirty-eight people in attendance to crane their necks and sigh at the sight of his exit. However, you know that those responses probably won't work because you don't want the person to doubt your abilities as a church planter or pastor. You certainly don't want them to feel bad for asking the question out of what appears to be a genuine concern.

So, you regroup in your mind and kick out one of your rote responses that involves you blathering on about some potential upcoming outreach or kids' ministry event. Maybe you even throw in the random new small group you hope to start soon, even though you're pretty sure that there's not one person in your small church capable of leading such a thing at the moment. Probably because they have cats too.

When I was dating my wife back in what now feels like the days of Lincoln, I made plans to visit her during her last semester of college at Auburn University. I'm a northerner who married a southern girl so each trip to Alabama was a real fun adventure for me. Maybe I was blinded by love, but I was genuinely fascinated by the south. People seemed way more interested in me and often took time to listen to my response before moving on to their next statement. In addition, the food was so good and the weather brought me a little more joy. I arrived in Atlanta where she picked me up at the airport and she surprised me with a trip to go see Jeff Foxworthy in concert.

Jeff Foxworthy is one funny man. His self-deprecating humor and storytelling is second to none. But what he is most known for is answering his own question, "You might be a redneck if…". For example, during our concert he said, "You might be a redneck if your retirement plan consists of scratch-off lottery tickets." Well, you might be a church planter if you've ever heard someone ask, "So how are you all doing?" I'm sure that most average church planters in North America can relate to the question and the difficulty of a response.

I remember taking a vacation sometime around year two in the life of my first church plant. We spent that first precious Sunday morning of vacation at the church where I used to serve just prior to planting. As a bit of background, when I left my staff position at that larger church in the south to go plant in the northeast, I became quite the head-scratcher to many in the congregation. I'm sure they were thinking to themselves, why would a fairly gifted and bright young man move his family to Pennsylvania and leave all this. In some regards this was still the days of, "Those who can't pastor, plant." I'm sure to many I was like Fonzie jumping the shark or Rocky getting in the ring with Ivan Drago.

After two years of slowly developing a core-team in our church plant in Pennsylvania and bringing our second child into the world we were basking in the fellowship of that Sunday morning. Vacation had given us a respite of warm Florida sunshine and people who snuggled our children and hugged us lovingly. Then the question came. Before I had a chance to grab my seat and feed once again under another pastor, the long-time greeter extraordinaire, Miss Bernice, caught me in a corner. "So, Larry, how are you all doing up there? How's the church going?"

Still green to the church planting thing and not knowing any better I joyfully responded, "You know, Bernice, it has had its ups and downs but we're good. We now have about 21 people on our team." My response was confident. That was good. My response dealt in numbers. That proved bad.

For the remainder of my life I will always remember Bernice's response because it has shaped my view of church planting, discipleship, metrics and success. She frowned just a little, glanced at my wife then turned back to me. Then as serious as a traffic stop she said, "Oh my. I knew when you left it was probably not going to work out." In that moment, every ounce of momentum, joy in ministry and confidence in myself and my calling felt like it was set on fire. The desire I had to worship the Lord that Sunday morning just had the largest bucket of ice water poured upon it. If not for my amazing wife slipping her arm around my waist, I might have hit the exit in Olympic speed.

Obviously, the statement hurt, and it forever created fear in me to be able to honestly answer someone who asks the earnest and sincere question, "So how are you doing?" But I was also able to use it, along with other uncomfortable questions like "So how many are you all running now?", to begin to have an honest conversation with God about what our metrics should look like as church planters. What timetable should you be on as a church planter? Which numbers matter most and should we be measuring other things as well? What defines my personal success and failure as a man of God? Is it wrong to step out and try something in faith even if it doesn't go according to your plan or someone else's plan? You see, the value I placed upon my life was based on metrics, and I wasn't even sure that the metrics were correct to begin with.

Stories and Spreadsheets

Like many pastors, my life prior to ministry involved another job and passion. I have always loved numbers and I was blessed to be able to spend four years studying business at Penn State prior to spending another three years working my way up in public banking and investing. While the call of God on my life to serve in pastoral ministry trumped my love for business, it did not wipe out my geeky passion for numbers. Numbers and spreadsheets to be more specific. I don't remember whether it was in high school or college that I was first introduced to spreadsheets, but watching numbers, formulas, and records at work is still like a healing balm to my brain.

When my wife informed me that she felt led to become debt free and she wanted to revisit our family budget to try and squeeze out a few more dollars to pay everything off I sprinted for the laptop. When our mission sending agency informed potential church planters that they would have to develop a funding strategy, I proudly held my printed spreadsheet aloft for all to see. I guess what I'm saying is that if you give me a number for just about anything, I will most likely turn it into a spreadsheet. And maybe if I'm feeling really adventurous, I'll spit out a graph as well!

The danger for me is that numbers can become just that … numbers. In my denomination we even add a spiritual spin to numbers by saying things like, "Numbers are noses and noses are people and people matter!" On the surface this is so very true. Numbers are people and people do matter; but time and time again I've wondered if our worth and success is based upon the people behind the numbers or the numbers themselves.

Hear me clearly when I say that numbers mattered to Jesus during his earthly ministry, but the numbers didn't dictate His ministry. More than numbers, the ministry of Christ was measured in human stories and individual life change. Christ had no building. What He did have were the homes of those who loved Him. Christ had followers that ranged in crowd size from just a few to thousands. Yet by the time of his death all but a handful had deserted Him.

We know that God considers numbers because the scripture gives us obvious examples of this. When the hungry crowds had swollen late in the evening in order to hear more of the master's teaching, the gospels deal in numbers:

> Now when it was evening, the disciples came to him and said, "This is a desolate place, and the day is now over; send the crowds

away to go into the villages and buy food for themselves." But Jesus said, "They need not go away; you give them something to eat." They said to him, "We have only five loaves here and two fish." And he said, "Bring them here to me." Then he ordered the crowds to sit down on the grass, and taking the five loaves and the two fish, he looked up to heaven and said a blessing. Then he broke the loaves and gave them to the disciples, and the disciples gave them to the crowds. And they all ate and were satisfied. And they took up twelve baskets full of the broken pieces left over. And those who ate were about five thousand men, besides women and children. (Matt 14:15–21)

This is fascinating on a number of levels. We are given exact numbers on how much food went into the making of this miracle; five and two. We are also given the exact number of leftovers; twelve. We are given the exact number of men or households; five thousand. Yet the numbers are not the most important part of the story. The five thousand most likely consisted of some who were earnestly seeking and some who were interested in the "show". The crowd was filled with disciples, antagonists and opportunists. So what do those numbers tell us? Not much.

This amazing work of Christ demonstrated his divine power and His authority over all things in order to care for the needs of His people; that's the bigger story than the numbers. The sufficiency of Jesus Christ is the bigger story. The bigger story is the stage being set for all mankind to recognize Christ as the bread of life, our manna from heaven. We can lose the significance of God's most telling traits because numbers have become the priority. Numbers matter, yet God is more than numbers and hence, so is His kingdom.

Allow me to draw your attention to one other example from scripture that may be even more relatable to a church planter. Consider the New Testament church just after Pentecost. Some truly amazing things are happening as documented in Acts following Peter's Spirit-filled sermon on that day when fire came and rested upon the believers in that upper room.

And Peter said to them, "Repent and be baptized every one of you in the name of Jesus Christ for the forgiveness of your sins, and you will receive the gift of the Holy Spirit. For the promise is for you and for your children and for all who are far off, everyone whom the Lord our God calls to himself." And with many other words he bore witness and continued to exhort them, saying, "Save yourselves from this crooked generation." So those who received his word were baptized, and there were added that day about three thousand souls. (Acts 2:38–41)

You can't get away from that number. It's a mighty big elephant in the text! Three thousand were saved and baptized that day. The number is so large that I have often wondered, as a pastor, how you logistically pull off a baptism service like that. Did the Apostles experience any rotator cuff injuries or have any numbness and tingling in their arms and back over the next couple of weeks?

Yet what can be lost somewhere under the foot of that massive elephant is, what I consider to be, some of the most important indicators of healthy church metrics still to this day:

> And they devoted themselves to the apostles' teaching and the fellowship, to the breaking of bread and the prayers. And awe came upon every soul, and many wonders and signs were being done through the apostles. And all who believed were together and had all things in common. And they were selling their possessions and belongings and distributing the proceeds to all, as any had need. And day by day, attending the temple together and breaking bread in their homes, they received their food with glad and generous hearts, praising God and having favor with all the people. And the Lord added to their number day by day those who were being saved. (Acts 2:42-47)

The numbers were actually a group of people behaving and living in a certain way that was starting to look a lot like the body of Christ. The scripture tells us that they were doing certain things that were causing other's outside the church to turn their head and take notice.

The church in Acts 2 appears to have been committed to one another. They disciplined themselves to meet regularly, break bread, and worship, pray and praise God together. They focused upon the teaching of the Apostles which at the time, prior to the written Bible, was the authoritative teaching of God. They focused on caring for one another even if it meant giving up something tangible of their own in order to fund the hardship of another. The scripture tells us that they lived thankful lives and that they were generous people.

And in turn, God did some pretty amazing things through them. God increased their witness through wonders and signs and God added to their numbers. It is clear that these were things that happened not as a result of some formulaic Christianity or a slick marketing campaign. They were not the result of a denominational program passed along at a mega-conference through some guy manning a booth in the hallway. They did not happen because one of the Apostles had peddled a tasty podcast the week before. These things happened because God did them. God added more and performed more miracles because He desired to do them in His time and in His might.

Which is more amazing? Three thousand people being saved in a single day or one woman cured of a lifetime of bleeding? Fifteen thousand or more people being fed on a hillside or a tax collector walking away from his wealth and sin? Jesus knowing that a woman had five husbands or Jesus setting that woman free from her sin and shame? I'm going to go out on a limb and say that all are amazing, but in our attendance driven, numbers driven culture we can lose the stories behind the numbers and in turn we can lose a true understanding of our value as a church and as a minister of Christ's gospel.

It's a Mindset

While planting my first church, God had to rework my heart on a lot of things and defining success would be top on that list. Like I mentioned, my only background in trained vocational ministry was in a larger church rooted in church growth. The church was absolutely amazing and lots of people were saved and lives were impacted for Christ, however, the first line of defining success was often some form of numerical growth.

Fast forward a couple years after arriving in our new mission field. My wife and I roll in at the appropriate time on a Sunday morning to a community gymnasium in Pennsylvania to begin setting up for church. As planters you make a lot of sacrifices and some of those are physical. I have the scars to prove it, and if you're a church planter I know that you do too. The gym where we met for worship was too big so we had to set up dividers. The gymnasium was on the first floor. All the chairs for the worship service were stored downstairs in the basement where the classrooms were also located. Along with a few of our volunteers, we would spend that Sunday morning, just like every other Sunday, hauling chairs upstairs and children ministry supplies downstairs.

Every Sunday was a lesson in humility as I would allow my mind to wander to the crowds that were probably gathering at my last church. I could smell the large coffee station outside the front door. I could hear the kids playing on the playground in front of the dedicated children's building. I visualized the pastors finishing up their corporate prayer time and rushing out to the foyer to shake as many hands as possible. And in my humility, I stood in that rented gymnasium lobby after doing everything I knew to do with as much excellence as we could muster and sip my cup of percolator coffee wondering if anyone would come. I stood at the edge of the parking lot all alone and prayed very hard each Sunday morning asking God to build His church by bringing people. I didn't know it at the time, but God was breaking some of my chains to old metrics and over the course of several years, He would build in my heart some new ones.

I was blessed with a wonderful core-team of about fifteen folks at the start of my first plant. These were truly amazing people who understood the vision and were sold-out to the mission work of church planting. They didn't need to be propped-up or noodled into the work, it just became like second nature to most of them. We would gather each Sunday morning after our launch (which is a whole other lesson in humility) and they would excitedly tell me about their week. They loved to share about who they met that week, how they had been praying, and how much the weekly bible study meant to them. They would even share how excited they were to make their famous dessert or baked beans for our Sunday evening F.I.S.H. (Fellowship In Someone's Home). Yet, shamefully, as they shared these wonderful aspects of their lives, I listened with one eye on the parking lot. It's like a crazy, wayward, scary, eye that can only focus on those things that increase numbers. It was an eye that was constantly focused on growing in numerical attendance yet remained blinded to the signs of healthy growth that were occurring right under my nose.

The measurement metrics were skewed during that early season of my church planting life. I would go home on Sunday afternoon and lament the fact that I was a failure to God and apologize to him for failing in his mission. My mindset was somewhere that was unhealthy and missing the full meaning of the Great Commission. If you are a pastor, you've probably preached it a million times to your congregations, small groups and church family but when was the last time you quoted the Great Commission to yourself as a pastor, planter or church leader? "And Jesus came and said to them, 'All authority in heaven and on earth has been given to me. Go therefore and make disciples of all nations, baptizing them in the name of the Father and of the Son and of the Holy Spirit, teaching them to observe all that I have commanded you. And behold, I am with you always, to the end of the age.'" (Matt 28:18–20) When you preach this text to yourself, you are forced to examine what is actually in the text and what is not.

Let's start with what actually is in the text: Living out the mission of Christ looks like disciples. Additional followers of Christ who are baptized, meaning that they are practicing obedience in their own lives as well as publicly declaring their faith to others. Disciples who are being taught the importance of adherence to Jesus' word. These are disciples who celebrate the word of God and personal righteousness in accordance with that word. In addition to disciples we see Jesus, right there at the beginning of the commission and at the end. He is the authority of the work and He is the support of the work.

Now let's take a look at what is not in the commission: church. The goal is making individual disciples and is not about making a church. Now before you castigate me or throw me out with the other anathema trash in your life, I want to clearly state that I understand that a church is made up of disciples. I get that in a big way. By faith I've hitched my livelihood to that wagon multiple times. I'm just asking the question regarding metrics and church planters. Are you making disciples who make a church or are you making a church? I believe there is a difference.

Where is your mindset as a planter? Is the end goal to fill a gymnasium or an auditorium or is it more? I like the way Jeff Christopherson put it when he asks, "If the sacred gathering is the exclusive and premier metric we track, we might want to rethink our motivation for planting a church."[1] It's not a bad thing to want people to come to your church or more specifically your worship service. I want them to come to mine as well. But why do you want them to come? Is there more to the Great Commission than filling seats? Do our own egos play into the metric at all? Are we basing our success upon having more filled seats than the church down the road or that of our pastor friend in a neighboring town?

Remember when I said that there were things that were not in the Great Commission? Well, allow me to be honest and give me a bit of leeway to mention one more thing: numbers. Jesus didn't say "Go and make twelve disciples a year." Nor did He say, "Increase your attendance by five percent each year." I don't know about you, but I find great freedom in that reality. Growth may be part of your mindset and part of your metric but a specific number doesn't add value or take away value in the eyes of Christ.

---

1. Christopherson and Lake, *Kingdom First*, 27.

God used my children to open my eyes to some of the long-term allegiances I had to metrics geared simply around size and numbers. There was a season early on in church planting when my denominational sending agency asked me to travel a couple of times a year to other churches and local associations of churches, to share all about the glamor and hard work that is North American church planting. During the three years that I received denominational support I was asked to go and share on maybe four or five occasions. There were a couple trips that I made on my own, but sometimes I would load up the family in the minivan and away we would go. Family vacations were precious those first few years, so we took advantage of as many opportunities to get away as possible. The excitement was palpable as we took these minivan getaways to tasty resort locations such as Marietta, GA and Cleveland, TN.

My children have spent most of their emotionally and spiritually formative years in church plants, so I was expecting lots of "oohs" and "aahs" as I took them to these larger churches with all kinds of crazy amenities. I thought the indoor rock-climbing wall in the children's building would be the topic of conversation for my seven-year-old after I was finished speaking. I thought my little daughter would giggle recounting the time she flew down the elephant trunk to enter her classroom which looked just like Noah's ark. I thought that they would marvel at the huge flat screens on the wall of the sanctuary. I thought I would catch my numbers-driven son silently counting every person in the seats. Much to my surprise, however, everywhere I went to speak, none of these things happened.

When we finally had time alone as a family in our car, I learned some very precious truths about my children and about their faith and their growth in Jesus. It wasn't that the things that they noticed at the larger churches weren't nice and even fun, but they didn't see the value of the church in light of those things. What they did see was people who loved church planters and their families. Earlier I mentioned the "stories" of people who encountered Jesus and how their lives had been changed. To this day, as a college freshman, my son can tell you the story of the man named Jack who listened to me speak on one of those trips. He can tell you how Jack was convicted of how he was wasting his money on lottery tickets and was led by the Holy Spirit to support our church planting efforts with his lottery ticket money in order to pay for my daughter's diapers each month. More than elephant trunk slides or crowd size, my son remembers the moving of God on the heart of that precious man. He remembers the work of discipleship and spiritual growth. In all my years of church plant-ing, this is one of the lessons that spoke loudest to me about what metrics are and how we should evaluate our work.

Playing the Comparison Game

It is human nature to look at others and make comparisons in all aspects of our lives. Whether you were in middle school wondering how your brand name shoes matched up to a friend's shoes, or maybe scanning the list of grades posted outside the professor's office in college, evaluating your grade against the rest of the class. Maybe you even find yourself aging a bit and wish you could look more like the latest, most handsome star on the big screen. If we are being honest, we think that when we assume a position of leadership that we will rise above this tendency to compare when in actual-ity, it probably tends to get worse. Comparisons can serve good purposes but can also tend to serve our sinful tendencies as well.

Playing the comparison game is, a bit like fishing. I grew up with a father that wanted to fish with me all the time. When I was ten years old, fishing was quite the chore because to my dad, fishing was a completely sedentary event in the most uneventful fishing locations. In other words, there was no movement and no thrill. It caused me to abhor the idea of fishing and led to some lost time with my dad. Around the age of forty, fishing became interesting to me again. This was probably due to the fact that my own body was beginning to slow down through normal aches and pains. My schedule, and that of my family, was also running me to the brink of craziness. Fishing offered solace much the same as sitting in a tree and hunting in the fall and winter. I was able to fish a few more years with my dad before he went home to be with Jesus, and it required me to relearn some things about fishing and learn a lot of new things.

Moving back to southwest Florida to plant a church at the age of 44 reminded me of the amazing fishing opportunities that surrounded me. One mile in one direction and I was fishing freshwater rivers, two miles in the other direction and I was fishing saltwater and some pretty big fish. The problem was (and still is) that I had very little idea what I needed to do to be most effective as a Florida fisherman. Usually, it is a little more involved than simply a bobber and a nightcrawler. So I employed the comparison approach to figure some things out.

I closely watched every other fisherman that I met in order that I might look at what they were doing compared to me. Terms like top-water lures, paddle-tail lures, cut-bait, and structure-feeders fed my vocabulary as I looked at other rigs and set-ups. I didn't know if they were better fisherman, I just knew that they were doing something that I wasn't. If I was catching catfish and someone was catching Spanish mackerel, I felt like I was failing.

Much like church planting, after a short period of time my enjoyment of fishing and my appreciation for each day on the water was being stolen by the feeling that I wasn't someone else. If you're like me, you have inevitably spent time speaking to someone that put out 400 chairs in a gym for their launch service. They told you spiritually heroic stories about how they prayed for weeks only to hear the Lord say to them, "Trust me!" So they praise God in between giggles as they recount their deep faith in God and how their worship team had to give up their seats because more than 400 showed up that first Sunday. Then there is you. You prayed really hard. You exercised every bit of intelligence, leadership and charismatic charm you could muster. You had your kids dragging out 75 chairs with great anticipation of how God was going to move in your midst as well. Then reality came down like a mighty thud! You realized your divine number wasn't 400, it wasn't even 75…it was 34.

You go home that Sunday afternoon working on spiritual-sounding responses for your sending church and your sending agency. Perhaps you groan or cry a little when no one is looking. You begin to pen your resignation letter so it sounds like you're not a complete and total moron. You try really hard to not take out your frustration on a pet or perhaps someone without fur like your wife. Yet deep down inside you hear this voice that says, "You're not like that other guy". Your mind may even begin to scripturally justify your failure by telling you that you are merely reaping the spiritual harvest in keeping with your talents. After all, didn't Jesus start that particular parable by saying, "To one he gave five talents, to another two, to another one, to each according to his ability." Now I'm not saying this is the correct exegesis of Matt 25:15, I'm simply firing off warning shots about how the dangerous game of comparison can torment our minds and hearts.

I've noticed that the sooner a church planter moves on from the comparison game and the evil tools that fuel it like Twitter, Facebook and Instagram, the sooner he will feel free to get serious about legitimate metrics.

The kind of metrics that indicate what God is doing on individual hearts, in their families, in their living rooms, and in their communities. The kind of metrics that speak to the health of the planter as much as the health of the church. At its basic level, comparison would never allow for a variety of new ways of planting because everyone would be trying to look just like the next church or mission. I like the way Jeff Christopherson stated the danger of striving for sameness when he said that lack of change in methodologies among church planting leaders led to "doubling down on a church planting idea that assumes a resident religious memory, but only to diminishing returns on our investment."[2]

After fourteen years of passionate laboring in the field of church planting, I have learned to root my metrics in biblical principles and examples rather than what other churches look like. I believe that there is a lot that we can learn from other's successes. We must study those successes, but, we must also temper it with the realities of our own God-given situations, communities and cultures. I have learned the freedom in being irregular. J. Oswald Chambers is one of my favorite authors on leadership and he emphasizes that importance of making room for the irregular leaders. In developing leaders like church planting missionaries, we should not throw away the irregulars because, "God has His 'irregulars,' and many of them have made outstanding contributions to world evangelization."[3]

Do you feel like an irregular? Do you feel like a powdered donut from Dunkin in a box of glazed Krispy Kremes? Do you feel exhausted when more programs and methodologies are handed over to you so that you can look like Grow and Go Coffee Church down the street? Do you ever wonder if the metrics that others are using to judge you are actually part of the sputtering and stalling of the church in the greater culture of our nation?

Just recently, I spoke with several friends who either pastor existing churches or serve on staff at existing churches. They all shared with me about their fears of what their churches might look like after the Covid-19 virus runs its course in the United States. They threw numbers out at me like 20 percent and 30 percent. That is how many people they fear might not return to the seats of their sanctuaries. I had the nerve to ask one friend whether he thought that those not returning was systemic of a metric

2. Christopherson, "Can We Now Agree that It's Time to Become a Different Kind of Church?", lines 12–14.

3. Sanders, "Spiritual Leadership", 150.

problem. If 30 percent won't ever come back to fill seats at your church, is filling seats the right metric to begin with?

It is my goal over the remaining chapters of this book to help you wrestle with metrics. You are more than free to disagree with me. Afterall, I'm married, so I'm used to it. I don't need every metric listed in this book to be your metric. I wouldn't be surprised by that because if you are planting a church you are probably irregular like me. I would be pleased, however, if it caused you to evaluate your church plant in light of scripture and dig into the hard places of what God might want to do in your new church.

Where is my heart?

Before we move on, it is important that you reflect upon your own heart in light of the work that God wants to do through a church plant. It is important to do some simple self-evaluation so that you might see yourself in the pages that follow as we highlight the not-so-ordinary work of church planting. Here is a list of some very basic reflective questions to help kick-start your true personal perceptions of church planting so that you can honestly assess the work that God wants to do through you and to be able to measure yourself by healthy biblical metrics rather than simply those which have been passed down from previous church movements and programs. Depending upon where you are in the church planting process, ask yourself the following rhetorical questions:

For current church planters:

1) Is my identity and worth as a Christ-follower somehow connected to the perceived success of my church plant?

2) Am I capable of viewing other churches and church plants as partners in the kingdom work?

3) Is the value of my Lord's Day determined more by attendance than personal worship?

4) Do the perceived successes or failures of my church plant directly relate to my ability to maintain a healthy home life?

5) Do I quietly have God tied to a timetable as it relates to some sort of perceived success or failure for my church plant?

6) Does attendance affect my ability to tend to my flock or core group?

7) Am I capable of regularly listing successes that are not tied to weekend worship attendance?

8) Does my spouse find joy in our church planting life?

9) Do I find myself constantly comparing my church plant to other church plants or existing churches?

10) Have I grown closer to Christ during my time of planting?

For potential church planters:

1) Do I have a hard time clearly articulating my call to church planting?

2) When I envision my church plant, is it God's church or someone else's?

3) Am I considering church planting with a backup plan in mind?

4) Who is confirming my call and who is lining up to partner with me?

5) Am I currently struggling financially?

I take great solace in Christ's simple yet very powerful statement in Matt 16:18 when He said, "And I tell you, you are Peter, and on this rock I will build my church, and the gates of hell shall not prevail against it." You don't build His church, He does. You are a faithful missionary. You are a church planter. You are not perfect and as such, your methodologies will not be perfect. Somewhere along our journey as the American church we have measured the success of established churches based upon numerical growth. While this may or may not be correct in certain circumstances, we have mandated it as the mark of a successful church planter as well. In the remaining chapters I pray that you are reminded of the extraordinary work of our extraordinary God and the simple, yet faithful, role that you play. If nothing else, may you be encouraged by who He is, and the work He wants to do in you and in your church, as well as the power of His word to set you free.

2

The Extraordinary Man

WE ALL HAVE HEROES. Those extraordinary people that we look up to and admire whether personally or from afar. Maybe they are secular giants that have really stood out in your life like monuments to greatness. Winston Churchill, John Kennedy, William Wallace, Lou Gehrig, or that volleyball that saved Tom Hanks' life in Castaway? Perhaps a teacher that put up with you in middle school and never really had the opportunity to see the model citizen that you turned out to be? (By the way, you should send that teacher a note today so that he or she can rest a little easier and stop paying for that home security system with your name on it.)

Like me, you may also have heroes of the faith: men or women who served their purpose under God and impacted the Kingdom in profound ways. When I think of my heroes of the faith, several giants come to mind. David Brainerd took the gospel to the Native Americans of Delaware and New Jersey despite constant struggles of hunger, loneliness, and sickness, eventually dying of tuberculosis. Martin Luther freed the truth of the gospel and all of God's word to the masses while staring down the juggernaut of religious authority known as the Catholic Church. Dietrich Bonhoeffer would not compromise God's church to the propaganda and oppression of the Nazi Party and Adolf Hitler. His life paralleled that of Hitler and his opposition eventually resulted in his hanging at a concentration camp in Flossenburg, Germany at the age of 39. Like so many heroes of the faith, what drives me to these three men is not what they produced for God but how they offered so much on the altar by faith to make themselves available to God. They were truly extraordinary!

With all that said, rarely do we think of ourselves as someone else's hero. We don't think of having the potential to be extraordinary in the eyes of another. As a church planter I have always felt more like a "master of painful toil" than that of a "hero". Yet much to my surprise, I discovered that I actually was a hero to another person – my son. Like many high schoolers, the fall of his senior year was consumed with multiple college applications and the essays that go along with each one. The essay questions can range from the simple to the bizarre (What hashtag best describes you?). In the midst of all this writing, a youth leader asked all the students to write a different kind of essay that challenged them to think of someone they view as a hero.

My son took pen to paper and shared how he looked up to me as a hero because his dad stepped out in faith to start two churches. He detailed how difficult it was at times but that his dad persevered. He shared how his dad often walked away from worldly success and opportunity in order to be obedient to what God had called him to do. It was a truly uplifting moment for me. Now don't get me wrong, he's still my son with warts and complications that would be familiar to every other parent. But his words gently washed over me with God's assurance that I wasn't a screw-up and that my own life, which I frequently would view as inconsequential, was actually extraordinary. It is extraordinary because of God in me and not because of merely size, numbers or some sort of programmatic success.

Tag! You're It!

God has a way of using some strange cats. I know, I'm one of them. As a young boy I was raised in a church that was light on biblical gospel teaching and evangelicalism, and heavy on tradition, stained glass, candles and elevated pulpits. My parents took me to this church until the age of ten. So many of my memories in that church consist of painful shoes, clip on ties, and the smell of damp linoleum in the basement where they stashed all the children for some form of childcare and Sunday School.

One image that does stand out clearly is the man behind the pulpit. Reverend Nettles was an imposing figure to a young boy because the man behind the elevated pulpit carried himself in a way that spoke of intimidation. You never really felt like he was speaking to you from the same level that you were on. He had a well-trimmed beard that any contemporary worship leader today would probably covet. Though he did not wear skinny jeans (Hey! It was the late 70's and early 80's) he did wear a dark black robe with frilly sashes and a strange frock sort of thing.

Everything in me looked at Reverend Nettles and saw someone who was unapproachable and floated on a cloud of spiritual arrogance. Nothing about him related to me. Now looking back, I'm quite confident that Reverend Nettles was not going for that vibe. He was probably a great guy who was down to earth. Perhaps the kind of guy that on Friday evenings would bowl a perfect game, woo your best girl right out from underneath you and talk smack about his mad Atari skills.

Fast forward a few years and you have a young teenage boy attending a new church where his parents made their new home. The vibe in the church itself was much more comfortable. The teaching was relatable and more focused on making disciples and reaching the lost. I am so thankful for that church because it was there that I heard about sin and the need for salvation through Jesus Christ. It was there that I repented and gave my whole life to the One who created me and died for me.

The church was led by pastor Jim. Pastor Jim cared so much for the people in his flock and worked really hard to love on them in very practical and tangible ways. I can remember when I left for college, my mom must have been pretty emotional for days. Pastor Jim called me at school on a phone that actually plugged into the wall and loudly rang with a noise that was nothing less than a stinging to the ears. When I answered, I was shocked that a pastor would take time to call a college kid over two hours away. He was worried about my mom and in turn worried about me. He wanted to make sure that I wasn't as homesick as my mom was for me. He took great care to ask the right questions and pray for me. I don't remember the exact words of that phone call, however, the call itself left an impression on me.

Sadly, so did Pastor Jim's socks. A year or so before I left for college, I was participating in a youth group event at the church. I think it was a cookout with a volleyball net set up in the grass. As a seventeen-year-old boy there was not one single sport that I was unwilling play. I worked hard to turn that youth group game into the cutthroat athletic spectacle that I desired. Just when I thought that the game was getting good, up strolls Pastor Jim. He asked if the pastor could join in. I get it now…he wanted to be hip, he wanted to be relatable, he wanted to be our pastor-friend. All I noticed at the time were his socks. His attire was a stained button-down shirt with short sleeves, khaki shorts, a wide brimmed sun hat, calf-high black dress socks and black dress loafers. I remember cringing and thinking, "There goes the athletic portion of this activity." Like I said, I was seventeen.

So later that year, Pastor Jim asked me to preach on "Youth Sunday". If you are blissfully ignorant to what "Youth Sunday" is, just know that it's when students are asked to lead the worship service and it is also the one Sunday when the pastor prays that visitors do not come in the door. Reluctantly, I agreed to preach. I learned a lot about how a concordance works and how little I actually had to say.

After I spoke, Pastor Jim came to me and said something so humbling and absolutely terrifying. He told me that he sensed a call on my life to preach God's word and pastor his church. In that very holy and humbling moment my mind went to two different men. My vision of being a pastor was Reverend Nettles in his robes and elevated pulpit as well as Pastor Jim's socks. I should have noticed other things like the calling they shared or the care that they exhibited, but my seventeen-year-old mind quickly informed God that this was not an option I would be taking Him up on any time soon.

Fast forward about seven years and I'm sitting in my office in a beautiful bank building in Sarasota, Florida. I had just taken a walk to the Gulf of Mexico over my lunch hour on a gorgeous day in February. Almost every day in February is gorgeous in southwest Florida but it is worthy of repeating. My phone rang and one of the customer service representatives in the office told me that she had a "Pastor Hal" waiting for me on the other end of the line. She didn't know it but on the other end of the line was a man about to do God's business with me.

Prior to that phone call, my life of inner peace and fulfillment had spiraled down into a place where only shadowy anxiety existed and joy was non-existent. I had recently confessed to my wife that I was having stomach issues that I'm pretty sure was tied to my anxiety. Most days I was stuck between Tums and a hard place. I hauled myself to work each day on zero motivation and somehow managed to pound out business that continued to increase my income and recognition in the bank. Yet despite the worldly success, I prayed to God that I wouldn't be doing this the rest of my life.

Pastor Hal was a family friend of my parents with a large personality and a lifetime of pastoring under his belt. When combined together, those two traits caused one to listen closely to every word that came from his mouth. After picking up the receiver and greeting him, we exchanged the normal perfunctory chit chat. Then, with little tact, he said to me, "So your mother tells me you're struggling physically and feel a little lost in life?" I admitted to my mother's assessment. Pastor Hal then asked me a question that changed the course of my life forever: "Son, how long are you going to run from God's call on your life?" It was the rudest, most in-your-face question I had ever been asked. It was also the key that opened the flood-gate to my heart and all that God sought to do in and through me. I was called. I knew it. Tag! I was now it! I told Hal he was right and more importantly that God was right. He shared more encouragement with me and then prayed with me while I sat in that bank office trembling.

I went home and told my wife, Mindy, what had happened and that I was called to be a pastor. Her response was as overwhelming as Hal's question. She simply said, "Well, it's about time you realized it." She had already been praying for me and considering how God could use me if I would simply submit. Called! I was called! But what did that mean? I played a lot of baseball in my young life and had been called out on strikes before (a lot). This didn't feel like that. I had been selected for leadership positions before. It didn't feel like that either. It was weightier and yet freeing all at the same time. I'm sure you can relate if you've experienced God's calling on your life as well. It's something that words can never fully explain.

It was a Wednesday, and I went to our prayer night at our church. Mindy and I sat around a circle with a few other church members where I shyly shared my revelation from that day and solicited prayer for what to do next. I was beyond confused at this point. Did I need to go to some special store and buy a robe? Did I need to contact the IRS? Should I buy a shirt and black socks like Pastor Jim? Should I sell stuff and pack up my wife and head off to seminary? Which seminary? Would they even want me?

As I asked for prayer, I felt two hands slip over my shoulders from behind. It was my pastor. He had been listening to my request and asked if he and his wife could stop by our little apartment to talk about what this meant. God had already begun to confirm my calling through my wife and by bringing a man into my life who would be a close mentor and friend to this very day.

Church Planting Metric One: Your Calling

I tell my story for several important reasons. First, I think it is always good to hear how God is still moving in the lives of men and women whom He chooses and calls to serve Him as He sees fit. There is a confidence in knowing that Jesus is still on the throne and that He is still moving on the hearts of others even when they're stubborn. In this day and age of disheartening news and churches closing their doors, we all need to be reminded, much like Elijah, that God still has for himself thousands of men who have not bowed a knee to Baal. (1 Kings 19:18)

Second, we don't talk about calling as much anymore. Men are leading ministries for a lot of reasons other than being called. Perhaps they have a nice wardrobe or hair. Perhaps they feel they are the most gifted or qualified. Perhaps they're the only one who has the guts to get up and speak for thirty minutes and then attest to the fact that no one fell asleep. Maybe they even like the idea of leading a group of people. While all of these things might be practical and useful, they do not matter if one is not called. J. Oswald Sanders put it best when he said, "None of these leadership qualities—dependence, approval, modesty, empathy, or optimism—are sufficient for the task. Without the touch of the supernatural, these qualities are dry as dust. And so the Holy Spirit comes to rest upon and dwell in the ideal Servant." Sanders also goes on to emphasize the fact that the same anointing that the Father offered to Jesus, He also offers to you.[1] These are heady words for sure, but important to be remembered as the hard work of church planting begins and later weighs heavy on your heart and mind. I've been called twice in my life. First was my call to pastoral ministry. Second was my call to plant churches.

Your Assurance

How confident are you in what God has called you to do? Strip away everything else and it is your lifeline. That's why I started with calling as our first metric. The Apostle Paul went through much. His ministry was one that we look upon now and consider it to be a wild success. In Paul's lifetime he might have simply referred to it as wild. I have a family member who serves in a ministry to many of the down and out families in and around Native American reservations in the southwestern United States. He recently shared how he has arrived at middle-age status having no hair on top of his head and a beard down his chest. He feels like he's failing in everything he does and even worse, with each passing day, he is more and more convinced that he has no idea what he is doing in ministry. He then said to me,

---

1. Sanders, *Spiritual Leadership*, 25.

"But at least I haven't been shipwrecked, imprisoned, beaten or stoned. I still have that going for me." Don't we all!?

In light of this, I have a news flash! You are broken as well. You are lacking skills and abilities. You are the wrong age, the wrong preaching style, the wrong size of family, the wrong family history and maybe even the wrong hair style. This is what makes you perfect. You are incapable apart from God. When speaking about the leaders that God uses, Dan Allender claims, "God loves reluctant leaders and, even better, he loves reluctant leaders who know they are frightened, confused, and broken."[2] This is great news for my family member who serves in ministry in the southwest and great news for every man who seems to have endless doubts about planting a church. Perhaps even more compelling, Allendar goes on to challenge the doubters with God's leadership model:

> he chooses fools to live foolishly in order to reveal the economy of heaven, which reverses and inverts the wisdom of this world. He calls us to brokenness, not performance; to relationships, not commotion; to grace, not success. It is no wonder that this kind of leadership is neither spoken of nor admired in our business schools or even our seminaries[3]

If you are honest in your 30,000-foot view of scripture, you would witness a cast of characters who look a lot like you and me and were used to do great things for God.

Ananias was a disciple of Jesus in Damascus during the early brutal days of this new movement we now know as Christianity. Persecution was a very real thing and Saul was one of the ringleaders. When God approached Ananias about going to meet Saul to deliver both sight and the Holy Spirit, you can probably understand his trepidation. But God's response to Ananias in Acts 9:15–16 is telling:

> But the Lord said to him, 'Go, for he is a chosen instrument of mine to carry my name before the Gentiles and kings and the children of Israel. For I will show him how much he must suffer for the sake of my name.'

I don't know if Paul knew of this job description ahead of time, if he did, you wouldn't blame him for thinking twice about accepting the job. Could you imagine God saying something to you like, "Joe, you will serve

2. Allender, *Leading with a Limp,* 53.
3. Allender, *Leading with a Limp,* 55.

me and I'll allow you to experience misery for my sake." If your name is Joe, you would probably start looking around for the nearest exit. Yet in these words we see the first key element to why the metric of calling is so important and such an assurance.

I have been around many church plants, and I have witnessed them grow and adapt under difficult circumstances. You can do without certain things and still maintain or grow a new church. However, without a church planter there will be no church plant. One important phrase from God's words to Ananias should jump out to us all: "a chosen instrument of mine". Knowing that assurance from God makes all the other stuff possible. By other stuff, I really mean complaining congregants, backsliding deacons, pandemics that kill any momentum, and volunteers that stop showing up because church planting is no longer glamorous. It is more like a slog through mud up to your knees. I understand that these things are not like a stoning, but on some Sunday afternoons they feel like it.

If you are not called to plant a church, then please do not plant a church. For the sake of the church, the witness of Christ in the community where you are thinking of planting, and most importantly for the sake of you and your family, don't do it. It is hard and you will want to quit at least once a week. When the stones come (and they will) and the crowds do not, what you'll be left with is your calling. I have personally watched several men confidently stroll into a new church plant still wrestling with the ability to communicate their call. Each man, after a period of time walked away with carnage in their wake including a bad reputation for Christ in their community, a bewildered and angry core group, or a family in tatters.

Your Spiritual Health

Church planting is a "big boy's" game. Do not allow yourself or anyone else to tell you otherwise. Everything you do will show up on Satan's radar. While your friends who pastor existing churches will tell their quips about how much they hate running deacons' meetings, you may not have one single deacon to walk alongside you for years. While those same friends tell you about how they prayed over the title to their next series of messages, you are going to be busy ordering a port-o-potty for a block party. While your needs and that of an existing church may seem quite different, the spiritual implications of what you are doing has not been lost on the Evil One.

I can remember in the early days my first church plant how excited I was to have a core team of fifteen people, including children, enlist themselves to make this new thing grow. I knew that some larger church plants started with many more, but these were very solid families. The first year and a half was spent reaching out to our community, engaging in missional activities as well as studying and fellowshipping in homes. It was beautiful. Then, due to differences, jobs, and homesickness, I woke up at the end of year two and half those folks were gone. We had added some others, but I was crushed. Had I not been spiritually growing and preparing myself for what was to come, I probably would have quit. I felt like I was living out Paul's words in Ephesians 6:16: "In all circumstances take up the shield of faith, with which you can extinguish all the flaming darts of the evil one". My perspective was never that our church was going to rise and fall on one event or one season, but more by how spiritually prepared and grounded I was for the long-haul. Jeff Christopherson bluntly put it this way, "When it comes to leading a church, especially a new church, character trumps everything. A long-standing church can often survive the calamity of a disgraced leader, but a new church rarely can. There is too much on the shoulders of a church planter."[4]

Your spiritual condition and the investment that you make in your own spiritual growth is going to play the largest role in the success or failure of your church plant. Others will tout you for your successful outreach to married couples or the warm, hip new lighting in your sanctuary, but your own spiritual health and strength is what will keep you on the pathway to long-term church planting success. Paul Tripp wrote a challenging book called *Dangerous Calling* where he pushes back against many cultural things that derail leaders in our church. In light of the conversation we're having about a called planter being a spiritually healthy planter, Tripp says: "You see, it is absolutely vital to remember that a pastor's ministry is never just shaped by his knowledge, experience, and skill. It is always also shaped by the true condition of his heart. In fact, if his heart is not in the right place, all the knowledge and skill can actually function to make him dangerous".[5] The effective leader is the one who is growing personally in Christ and leading out of that overflow rather than simply based upon temporal results and/or talents.

---

4. Christopherson, *Kingdom First*, 33.
5. Tripp, *Dangerous Calling*, 62.

Many Sunday's I come home after a small group meeting or a worship service and wrestle with failure. I remember one time I worked with a few other volunteers to make some improvements in our sanctuary that I thought would make it more inviting. The following Sunday a church member pulled me aside after church and informed me that whoever had that idea failed miserably. Maybe you've been there? Yet despite this, I continue to think to myself that if I could just do this one thing or magically make something else happen, I'll be successful.

A spiritually healthy church planter is never going to evaluate themselves based upon ministry successes and failures because their spiritual walk with Christ is going to ground them in who they really are. You do not need to establish a booming church plant that either you or another entity defines as successful in order to be loved in the eyes of God. Peter Scazzero in *The Emotionally Healthy Leader* notes that one great sign of an unhealthy leader is the one who tries to lead from their doing rather than their being. He further offers that an unhealthy leader refuses to accept the notion of "slowed-down spirituality".[6] Take time to remember where your calling comes from and then allow Christ to lead out of your strong and healthy relationship with Him.

One side note to add for the purpose of spiritual health. Paul warns Timothy that an overseer "must not be a recent convert, or he may become puffed up with conceit and fall into the condemnation of the devil". (1 Tim 3:6) This is a warning against a danger in the opposite direction. A recent convert may not have the spiritual maturity to handle "quick success" in a church or church plant. You can probably recall some of the train-wreck stories of pastors and/or planters who began to spend more time reading their press clippings than the word of God. Paul Tripp, with brutal honesty, put it best: "Your ministry will be shaped by worship of God or worship of you or, for most of us, a troubling mix of both."[7] Make sure that you are prioritizing your own spiritual depth and maturity before you try to take an entire church to that place.

Your Physical Health

As if church planting couldn't be any harder, throw in a frail, broken tent that we call a body. I have done more physical things in the name of planting

6. Scazzero, *The Emotionally Healthy Leader* 31.

7. Tripp, *Dangerous Calling,* 167.

a church than if I simply pastored an existing church. If you are not careful you can become oblivious to your physical health in an effort to fulfill your calling and mission.

Most church planters will probably attest to the fact that you will chase down any opportunity to reach your community. This also means that because you're the church planter you will put in the most prayer, the most time and often the most physical effort to accomplish these opportunities. I have clear memories of missing three meals in a row in order to make a block party happen. I remember sitting sixty plus feet in the air after dark, cleaning out gutters following storms and floods that ravaged our neighborhood. I remember unhooking a trailer that we used for a service project in the dark during a cold late-winter evening. The hitch-lock became frozen and so I chose to use a hammer to clear it. I missed the hitch-lock and found my thumb. Blood stains in my truck were evident for a long time after that. I remember being so worried about losing momentum in ministry that I insisted on holding services after a snowstorm only to fall down my own driveway on ice cracking the back of my skull on the blacktop. When I turned thirty I got glasses. Thanks to church planting, when I turned thirty-five I got a concussion.

When I left banking to pursue my call to ministry, I was 6'2" tall and about 190 pounds. Now, I don't know if you've been around church ministry, but food is often involved … a lot. After seven years in ministry when I left to pursue my call to church plant, I was up to approximately 205 pounds. Fast forward four years into my first church plant and I was now 220 pounds. Clearly this was not a good trajectory. In my mind's eye, I once resembled Captain America but was now looking more like Kung Fu Panda. I had become an emotional eater, an irregular eater and a ministry eater.

These are not stories that I tell you to draw attention to my own woes as much as I wish to simply scare you. Planting a church is a physical game. It can also be a hard game. You will insist that you are too busy in ministry to care for yourself. The only person you'll be cheating with that mentality is yourself and your family when you die prematurely.

Discipline yourself to rest and exercise and eat right. Scazzero also notes that another sign of an emotionally unhealthy leader is the person who cannot practice Sabbath which he calls a "weekly, twenty-four hour period in which they cease all work and rest, delight in God's gifts, and enjoy life with him."[8] There will be times when you need to go away. You will need to seek God in your life. Not more ministry ideas, but simply Christ.

Sabbath rest wasn't occurring early on in my church planting days. I felt I was too important and too "disciplined" to need such a thing. After all, isn't every day as a pastor supposed to be a workday? No. I had become frustrated, bitter and ready to quit. I was exhausted spiritually and physically. My wife booked me a hotel room at one of my favorite places for two nights and told me that I need to learn to rest again. It wasn't a posh hotel, but it was in Gettysburg. She knew I would walk outside, journey ancient battlefields and dwell on things other than ministry. She was right. I came out of those two days refreshed with a new understanding of Sabbath. From that point on I have always cleared one day a week for at least one full twenty-four hour period to do zero church work (barring an emergency of course) and focus on simple joy in Christ and his gifts.

You should use those days to do things that bring joy and then don't feel bad about it. I learned to hunt again. I learned to fish. I stole my children out of school to hop a train to baseball games. And in keeping with the weight issue, I learned to run. Running became a therapy, a hobby and a life-changer. I dropped thirty pounds and ran six half-marathons. As I age, the miles aren't the same, but the therapy is. Find your sabbath and guard your physical health so that you can be wired for the long-haul.

Church Planting Metric Two: Your Family

My son is currently a freshman at the University of Florida. I often joke that he is one of the smartest people I know in real life. I have loved every day with him. When we packed up our life to go plant our first church, I remember clicking his four-year-old body into his car seat in the back of the old Saturn. Remember Saturn? Those were the days. I'm now knee-deep in my second church plant and I would give anything to have him clicked into that car seat one more time teaching me sign language from the back seat. The years with your church plant might be hard but the years with your family are fast. Your family is your safe-place and your first ministry. So important is your family that God lists it as a qualification for those seeking to lead his church, including the hippest and coolest of the church planters.

---

8. Scazzero, *The Emotionally Healthy Leader*, 32.

> Therefore an overseer must be above reproach, the husband of one
> wife, sober-minded, self-controlled, respectable, hospitable, able
> to teach, not a drunkard, not violent but gentle, not quarrelsome,
> not a lover of money. He must manage his own household well,
> with all dignity keeping his children submissive, for if someone
> does not know how to manage his own household, how will he
> care for God's church? (1 Tim 3:2–5)

There is a lot in this text that can scare a man clean out of the pulpit
and ministry altogether. Based upon this job description one might think
that God doesn't really want anyone to serve as a pastor/elder. I would say
that it serves as a warning that God doesn't want "just anyone" to serve as
pastor/elder. The man of God, called to plant and pastor Christ's church is
to be an extraordinary man with an extraordinary call. The household of
that man is evidence of such a life.

Your Wife

I live in a semi-tropical climate in southwest Florida. What that means is
that for five to six months out of the year it rains almost every day. Sometimes it lasts ten minutes and sometimes it will last for hours with lightning
that will curl your toes and make you think twice about angering God. Living in this climate also means that we can get some pretty dry stretches during the winter months. I love sunshine and 75 degrees every day in January
but eventually my lawn hates it. So I quickly learned the importance of
having and maintaining an irrigation system so that I can in turn go out
and mow more and more.

When my irrigation system goes bad and I need to fix it I inevitably
call my father-in-law. A long-time Floridian and grass connoisseur, he has
fixed it all. Many Floridians pay fancy companies to come out and do these
kind of repairs, however, I'm a church planter and I'm habitually cheap.
It was during one of these repair episodes that I learned about PVC and
solvent cement. In order for two pieces of PVC plumbing to seal properly
two agents are required. First, the connection point should be coated with
a primer, followed by the solvent cement. These two react with a slight increase in temperature causing a very effective, tight seal in the two PVC
pieces.

So important to the life and ministry of a church planter is his wife,
like a solvent cement, he would be a leaky, ineffective sieve without her. The

minister of Christ must model the prioritizing of this special lady in private above all else. How quickly we forget that the best that our ministry message has to offer is no better than the strength of our marriage. Peter Scazzero refers to the fact that married couples "bear witness to the depth of Christ's love".[9] He then builds upon this idea proposing that if you want to lead out of your marriage, then your marriage, not ministry, must be your first passion and "loudest gospel message".[10] You cannot have a healthy church plant if you do not have a healthy marriage. Notice that I didn't say perfect marriage. There is no such thing, and if there was, you wouldn't be in it.

Likewise, you cannot have a healthy church plant if your spouse is regularly placed upon that sacrificial altar of ministry. If this becomes your practice, you will lose a spouse and a church. About one year into my first church plant it became clear to me that the hardest obstacle wasn't reaching the lost or making budget. The hardest obstacle was the battering that we were receiving in the midst of disintegrating personal relationships. As a man, I found myself compartmentalizing, brushing aside and overlooking comments and strains. My wife was internalizing, crying and dying on the inside. After a particularly bad day, we put our children to bed and settled in to watch American Idol (don't judge me). Rather than turning on the television, Mindy just sat there and stared off into the paint color of the wall. Tears streamed down her cheeks. My Mindy rarely cries.

I grabbed her hands as she crumbled into a heap on the floor. I thought I had wronged her or that she received bad news to which I wasn't aware. In one of the most pointed statements that she ever made to me, she looked up through her tears said, "If planting a church for Jesus means going on like this, promise me that you'll take me away."

My wife has always been my rock, she is my cement compound and my biggest cheerleader. Those words brought the reality of my ministry to her to the top of everything that I held sacred. I didn't have to pray about my response. I didn't have to consult any trusted advisors. I squeezed her hands, drew her in to hug her and said, "I promise."

I understand the doctrinal debate about 1 Tim 3:2 and "the husband of one wife". I'll allow other theologians to opine on the issue of divorce and physical adultery. My concern for you, church planter, is that the church you plant doesn't become your first ministry and that it doesn't become

---

9. Scazzero, *The Emotionally Healthy Leader,* 87
10. Scazzero, *The Emotionally Healthy Leader,* 92.

your mistress. Jesus will not be honored in that. Make sure she knows that you have one wife.

Your Children

Maybe you're like me and compared to your wife, your kids are a bit of a wildcard. At least your wife chose you at one point and time. She took a ring, walked an aisle, made a vow. Your kids just kind of showed up. I mean, you hopefully knew at some point that they were on their way. They didn't just land on your doorstep with ratty luggage begging for more porridge. But they didn't have a say in choosing you. They're stuck with you. The good, the bad and the ugly.

When my children were very young, I would read Paul's words to Timothy and laugh outwardly at the prospect of "managing" them well or keeping them "submissive". It seems like a losing prospect in your own strength. Social media hasn't made it any easier. When I first logged onto social media my oldest was six and my youngest was one. I immediately began to notice that everyone's life on social media was better than mine. All parents were rockstars, Christian parents were posting pictures of little Suzy or Johnny getting stickers for memorizing Deuteronomy after their homework was finished. Is that who I needed to be as a parent?

I learned along the way that there is no such thing as a perfect parent just like there is no such thing as a perfect family. We "manage" along the way by positioning our children, with a pleasant manner, how to submit to authority. We demonstrate our own submission to God's authority in our life so that as they reach adulthood, they strive to do the same. As we planted our church our children joined us in those rhythms. I think this is why I love the Shema, where God reminds his people to teach his word to their children "when you sit in your house, and when you walk by the way, and when you lie down, and when you rise." (Deut 6:7) Our children have learned submission through our teaching and through our example.

It is also important for your children to know that you prioritize their lives ahead of your church plant. When we planted our first church, our children were part of a fairly large group of other children in our core team. They fit into a ready-made children's ministry. The second time we planted a church it was with a teen and a tween and no substantial youth group. We decided as parents that we would drive thirty minutes north each week to our sending church so that our children could have some time growing with peers in a strong youth ministry that had strong biblical teaching. I'm not saying that your children need a youth ministry. However, study your children and know what they need, then do it. This is what it takes to manage your household well.

Your Financial Health

If you're like most pastors you do not enjoy talking about money, and you especially do not enjoy talking about your money. If you're like the majority of pastors you're probably chuckling to yourself right now and saying, "Sure, what money?" Extravagant for you is probably lunch at Cracker Barrell. I get it. Yet Paul's words to Timothy still stand as a check on our hearts to this day, perhaps more than ever. The man God calls as an overseer must not to be a "lover of money".

It is roundly shared that the condition of a pastor's family and his finances are consistently listed as two of the top reasons for the failure of new church starts. In today's day and age where church planting is often viewed as glamorous, one could easily see planting as a way to fame and fortune. After all, most of the planting programs you subscribe to, planting conferences you attend and planting books you read are going to be spearheaded by highly successful, well-traveled, polished planters who saw their churches explode and now have lots of things you might want.

The opposite side of the same coin is the planter who struggles financially. The majority of planters, like me, are going to spend many years living in financial mediocrity while your ministry friends and partners go on more elaborate vacations and talk of nice retirement accounts. You can easily begin to resent them or feel entitled to what God has given them.

My advice to you is simple: make sure you are prepared to live on what your church planting situation allows you. If you feel that not having enough financially could lead you to a place of sin, then don't plant that church. Before planting a church, my wife and I spend time in prayer asking God what we need financially as a family. We fashion a family budget in light of a church plant budget and commit to live within that until God grants an increase. At the risk of sounding super-spiritual, we pray and ask God to blind us to the affluence of others and rather, find our contentment in His hand.

Show me a man content in his home life, leading his family well and managing his finances well and I'll show you a man who is well on his way.

Maybe you are plugging along as a planter. Maybe it's year three and you just had your first baptism. Maybe you just watched a key family from your core group leave because they needed a bigger-budget ministry. You lock up the small space where you meet each Sunday, you take the trash out to the curb because trash runs on Mondays, and you head home to your wife who loves you so much. Your children tell you what they and the two other kids made in Sunday School and you smile. Your sweet wife informs you that a leftover meatloaf sandwich is for lunch and you get excited. I'm telling you planter…you're doing just fine.

3

The Extraordinary Power

I GREW UP IN an urban environment and made the most of it. While some may have spent their childhoods on horses or wading in creeks, I spent mine playing stickball, swimming in public pools, walking to the afternoon matinee and building go-carts to race in the streets. My father was a police officer and most of my friends knew him, respected him and found him to be quite entertaining. It wasn't unusual for my father to come home on a summer evening and stick his head out the back door and whistle. His whistle was amazing! On a ranch they might have a dinner bell, well in the west end of my hometown there was Officer Snyder's whistle. Like a call of the wild, I would hear it blocks away and instinctively know that it was time to sit down for dinner. And even if I didn't hear it, sure enough, one of my friends would hear it and relay the notice to me. We didn't have much, but on those summer afternoons it was a charmed life.

One of the ways we would occupy our time on those summer days was to reimagine our bicycles. Sometimes it was a complex reworking, with a new seat we found in someone's garbage or installing a new chain. Sometimes it was as simple as installing a new motor. Well, not really a motor, it was a playing card. The card was taped to the frame of the bike and interlaced between the spokes and when the bike rolled – the sound of an engine filled the air. If we desired the sound of a Harley, we simply took more cards from the deck. By adding more cards, ours bikes gave the audible appearance of a powerhouse, yet the moment that big hill in the next neighborhood came into view, we realized that all we had was a hand-me-down Huffy with a banana seat.

In the world of church planting, there is real danger in trusting in things of appearance rather than power. Much liking taping playing cards to a bicycle and trusting in the noise to power it up the hills, planting in the power of yourself will prove as equally exhausting as it is ineffective. Granted, I do not know your depth of personality and charisma. I have no idea how articulate you are as a communicator. I have not taken a serious look at your outstanding marketing plan. I do not even fully comprehend your polished style of dress or the size of your core group. I'm simply saying that you alone cannot build a church and you cannot do it on gifts, things, or particular circumstances by themselves.

Settle on a General Contractor

In my previous life as a banker I had multiple opportunities to write construction loans for some wonderful people who were literally putting their dreams in concrete. I learned a lot about the home construction process. I learned that each new home has a general contractor who ultimately answers for the whole process and finished product. He or she may have some subcontractors who handle the electrical work or pour the slab but when push comes to shove, the general contractor answers for it. So if I was a subcontractor and decided that I wanted to shortcut something or put my handprints in the wet concrete, I might have to answer to the general contractor, but he or she would have to answer to the bank, and the customer, and maybe even a licensing board.

Ultimately it is the general contractor who builds your house, calls the shots, and puts their name on it. My wife and I had one opportunity to build a house during the earlier years of our marriage. Our son was two and we wanted a bit more space. A general contractor in our church really wanted to build us a house, but we were afraid that it would always remain out of our price range. After speaking with him he made sure that we could afford the house. What a blessing!

I remember at one meeting with him we were looking at exterior elevation plans and he felt like the outside of the home needed to look "beefier". "I want my pastor to have a house that looks stout from out front," he said with conviction. He told me how he was going to raise the roof a bit, throw a couple columns in the front, and put a larger window over the garden tub. It was like he was speaking a foreign language to two young pups on a small income. Yet here is the amazing thing, he was the general contractor and he made it happen. Every time I walked in my front door, I would think to myself, "I love my beefy house!"

I think the safest place for a church planter to be is in a similar place with regard to Christ and his church. Consider the wonderfully high point in the gospels when Jesus takes his disciples to Caesarea Philippi, a region north of Galilee near the base of Mount Hermon, a region which we refer to today as the Golan Heights. While there, Jesus began to question his disciples about who others said that he was. The disciples all proffered answers including Elijah and John the Baptist. Then Jesus changed his questioning a bit to make it more personal for them in Matt 16:15–19.

> He said to them, 'But who do you say that I am?' Simon Peter replied, 'You are the Christ, the Son of the living God.' And Jesus answered him, 'Blessed are you, Simon Bar–Jonah! For flesh and blood has not revealed this to you, but my Father who is in heaven. And I tell you, you are Peter, and on this rock I will build my church, and the gates of hell shall not prevail against it. I will give you the keys of the kingdom of heaven, and whatever you bind on earth shall be bound in heaven, and whatever you loose on earth shall be loosed in heaven.'

Peter's confession is like that watershed moment that you've been waiting for in a movie. Like when Coach Devine finally puts Rudy in at the end of the game or when Forrest Gump learns for the first time that he has a little Forrest. The question went from "who do other's say?" to "who do you say I am?" This was Jesus concerning himself with their hearts. Peter, in a moment of spiritual clarity blurts out the truth. Jesus is the Messiah and God's Son. This is to be the core teaching of the church and one we will discuss more in the next chapter.

It is Jesus' response that should be telling to every pastor, ministry leader and church planter. Jesus says two important facts: First, he says to all that are listening and to us today that he is the builder of the church. Second, he refers to the foundation of the construction which is faith.

You Can't Plant a Church Like Rosie Ruiz

Do you know who won the 1980 Boston Marathon for women? If you answered Rosie Ruiz, you would be both right and wrong. It's not a trick question. Maybe like millions of Americans who view running as a form of plague that only wiry, sadistic people endure, you don't even care. However, those who trained long and hard to finish any type of long-distance foot race know who Rosie Ruiz is, and they care quite a lot.

Ruiz decided that the race itself did not matter, rather, the only thing that mattered was the finish. Upon finishing first and being interviewed by the press, many other runners and commentators began to notice that she didn't have knowledge of her own time intervals, lacked a sweaty appearance, and seemed to even lack the physique of an elite champion marathon runner. It was later discovered that the opportunistic Ruiz jumped out from the crowd with a little less than a mile remaining in order to be recorded as a finisher. Problem was, she did not pay much attention to who passed by or what the times were, so she ended up jumping ahead of every woman in the race finishing at a blistering pace (if it were true). Ruiz was later found out and it was only the beginning of the crumbling to her house of cards

She qualified for the Boston Marathon by completing the New York City Marathon in which (you guessed it) she pulled the same stunt. Perhaps even more appalling, Ruiz qualified for the New York City Marathon by exemption, claiming that she was dying of brain cancer, which she was not. Rosie Ruiz believed that if she cut enough corners and skipped the endurance part, she could be viewed as one of the elites. The truth found her out.

There will be at least two great temptations when planting a church. First will be the temptation to abandon what you believe about making disciples in order to grow faster. Second will be the temptation to quit when things are moving slower than the expectations of those around you and perhaps the desire of your own heart.

Church Planting Metric Three: Faithfulness

Years ago, I was sitting in a seminary class for church planters. I had seven years of vocational ministry under my belt. I was about to transition into the next phase of life which centered upon planting my first church somewhere in south central Pennsylvania. My mind and my heart were already wrestling with expectations that were beholden to the church growth movement while also wondering if authentic discipleship always had to be evidenced by huge attendance numbers.

During a particularly healthy time of discussion, a fellow planter and classmate said something that has resonated with me ever since. He simply stated, "I believe that God is more interested in developing faith than fruit." Now to be honest, the catchy alliteration probably made it even cooler, but the statement stuck with me and caused me to think scripturally. Was this true? Is the God of the Bible in need of some fruit that we produce or is he looking to grow me into a person of faith?

Church planting is by far the most difficult thing I have ever done in my life (twice). It requires a level of commitment and long-term vision that only faith can sustain. It demands a sustained focus from not just you, but those you lead in a core group and later in a congregation. Church planting will leave you with doubts, heartaches, struggles, and challenges. In my unscientific personal observation, difficulties seem to outnumber victories at a rate of four to one. Yet, consider the words of J. Oswald Sanders when speaking about leadership: "While others lose their heads, leaders stay the course. Leaders strengthen followers in the middle of discouraging setbacks and shattering reverses."[1] Most days you will be tested in your faithfulness and courage in Christ. Don't be afraid to evaluate how you're doing at simply remaining faithful to the call and vision God has given you.

Taking Matters into Your Own Hands

In First Samuel we read the story of Israel's first king named Saul. Twice he concerns himself more with results than faithfully trusting in God's plan and timing. In First Samuel 13, Saul is pinned down at Gilgal by the Philistines, the same enemy God promised to help them defeat. Rather than waiting on the priest, Samuel, to make an offering, Saul takes the responsibility upon himself. The results were brutal. When Samuel finally arrives, he informs Saul of God's judgment, "your kingdom shall not continue." (1 Sam 13:14) Talk about blunt honesty and immediacy of judgment!

This would not be the end of Saul's lessons. Later in First Samuel 15, Saul takes down the Amalekites through the power of God. God instructs Saul to completely destroy everything belonging to the Amalekites sparing no thing or person. Saul again fails to trust God at his word. He holds back some fruit for himself in the form of the best of the spoil. Once again Samuel arrives with words of rebuke declaring, "Has the Lord as great delight in burnt offerings and sacrifices, as in obeying the voice of the Lord? Behold, to obey is better than sacrifice, and to listen than the fat of rams." (1 Sam 15:22) Fruit is what you lay on the altar. But according to God, faithfully trusting and obeying is greater than any fruit that you might throw down on the altar.

1. Sanders, *Spiritual Leadership*, 61.

37

Believe me when I tell you that I get it. I wrestle with it each and every day. Like the church planter reading this somewhere, I too have thought, "if I just steal a few sheep in my own strength, then our church will arrive at the status or footing that we have been working so hard for." I too have thought, "I'm going to deliver up a congregation of 200 people to Jesus in three years and then I will have arrived at a point of divine favor." I have also cried my heart out to God at least once a week wondering what in the world He is up to and why everything seems to result in abject failure.

Much like the leader, Saul, we easily forget that the faith that we are learning to cling to in our own lives is also what we are teaching to those who follow us. Your core group, your small congregation, is learning what it means to wait on God based upon your responses to God's timing. For years, much of American church culture has been led to believe that bigger is better or more expensive is better. The problem is that little thought was given to how a church arrived at "bigger" or "more expensive". Allow me to illustrate this point using church discipline.

It is 1996 and Rising Behemoth Church on one side of town is really cranking. In the past two years they have increased Sunday attendance from 150 people to about 500. There is no membership class or personal expectations, but the pastor of missions and social justice at Rising Behemoth has led the church to start producing their own brand of "Fair Trade" coffee that they serve each Sunday for $2.25 a cup. The money goes to make sure that farmers in Columbia are not being short-changed by larger, greedy American coffee corporations. The church is hip, and the music is spot on and the bar of expectations for Jesus disciples is set low.

On the other side of town is Struggling Disciples Church. They've only grown from 35 to 50 in that same period of time. The pastor and church planter at Struggling Disciples Church is a man named Mark. Mark has long been committed to not just growing in size but also growing in discipleship. He has implemented a vision to see members working with other members to increase their witness and accountability. The process is painful because it is hard work. It seems like each step they take forward in attendance, they fall one step back as someone slips out the back door.

Roger used to attend Struggling Disciples Church with his wife, Tara. Tara confided in a discipleship partner one evening that she just found out that Roger has been having an affair for thirteen months with a woman outside the church. In keeping with Pastor Mark's vision, several men went to Roger to address the situation with him and seek repentance and restoration. In a furious rage, Roger refused the rebuke as well as correction and chooses to leave the church and Tara. Three months later, Pastor Mark learns that Roger and his mistress are now attending Rising Behemoth. Mark calls to speak with the pastor at Rising Behemoth to warn them of Roger's infidelity and the start of church discipline. Mark's call is never returned. Roger now sings on the worship team at his new church.

The point of this all-too-real example is NOT that bigger or more expensive is evil or wrong. The point is that, if not careful, we all can be tempted to utilize Rosie Ruiz or King Saul tactics to arrive at the results that we want rather than trusting in the biblical expectations that God places before us. Through the years much has changed in both secular and church culture. The one constant has been the pressure to look like the church down the street as quickly as possible thus proving our church to be viable and relevant. Pastor, Planter or Team Member – don't measure yourself by speed or by the size of construction. Don't be tempted to measure your church by relevance or crowds. First ask yourself if you are faithful to what Jesus is seeking to build. It is his church, and rest assured, he is interested in building a biblical, disciple-making church. But more on that later.

The Ugly Truth About Faithfulness

Jeff Christopherson, in his outstanding book, *Kingdom First,* states, "The point is not to have a fast-growing church; the point is to have a healthy church that is positioned to grow and eventually multiply. And regardless of the model of your church plant, if you want to have a healthy and growing church, you must first have a healthy and growing team."[2] Through the years I have employed several key tactics that have forced me to stretch my faith in an effort to remain faithful to the biblical church that God desired to build through the team that he brings. The first tactic is a brutally honest conversation with any individual, couple or family wishing to get involved in our church plant early on. Second is a brutally honest conversation with many Christians who are quickly transitioning from another church. Third, to prioritize each and every person as a member of the kingdom ahead of being a member of my church.

The first brutally honest conversation is pretty hard in the beginning stages of your church. You want to take any human being with a pulse in the early days to bulk up the foundation of what you're doing. I've read all the

2. Christopherson, *Kingdom First*, 140.

stuff where the planting experts encourage you to load up those numbers in the beginning anyway you can. Create that illusion of size and reap the rewards later on. Put your six-year-old in a booster seat in the back row if necessary. However, just speaking honestly from experience, I've been heartbroken many times when those I've thrown into the mix in the beginning or acquiesced to their small demands, walked out when you faithfully walked where Jesus called you to go as a planter. Planting a church is hard.

I can remember sitting in coffee shops or on the phone with potential planting team members as they told me how much they wanted their family to be a part of what our plant was seeking to do. All smiles in the beginning, I honestly tell them that their two-year-old and seven-year-old may be in the same class for a year or two as we grow due to lack of available teachers. I honestly tell them that we won't have our own youth group early on and may need to link up with a partner church. I honestly tell them that they will be needed to serve in areas where the need is great, and their comfort level is not. I honestly tell them that church planting is hard and it is missional and, in many ways, it is not about their needs.

The faithful will jump on board despite those hard conversations and you put a check next to your metric. Those who may not be comfortable with such difficulties in a church or who were not expecting such challenges will move on. That's okay as well. You faithfully trusted in what Christ was building and you put a check next to your metric.

The second brutally honest conversation can actually be more difficult than the first. One thing you'll notice as a church planter is that you and your missional church will become a magnet for certain types of people. I like to refer to them as the "runners" and the "needers".

Runners will be those who see your church as a place they can run to in order to escape the circumstances, deficiencies or uncomfortableness of their last church. Typically, they are running from a problem or issue that has caused them pain or made them anxious. They will say things like, "we felt it was important to be someplace smaller where the pastor could be more attentive." They also might say, "the worship team at our last church didn't appreciate my musical gifts." Runners tend to continue to run and early church plants are not a healthy place for runners. So, look down, and if they have worn out running shoes, do not be afraid to question them with honesty. You may want to warmly warn them that a church plant is going to require putting that which makes you uncomfortable or frustrated to the side.

Needers come in two basic flavors. There will be those people who love to tell you how much you need them. They will list all the areas where they noticed that you are deficient. (Usually these areas are of little importance to you.) They will say things like, "I just want you to know that I have a lot of skill at installing sound boards and lighting racks." They may also say things like, "We feel blessed to be able to give large financial gifts. Surely this would benefit your church." Or my personal favorite, "I noticed you don't have anyone to play the timpani drum. I sure feel like I could be used by the Lord. Can I store my drum at the church?" This last question comes after you just explained the reality of set-up and tear-down each Sunday morning.

One challenge to the needer's desires is that often what ties the smaller church together is not what the needer wants to highlight from their last church experience. Church growth expert, Gary McIntosh noted in his research that most churches under 200 in attendance shared a common denominator of focus on relationships.[3] The smaller churches are known more for mutual love and doing life together rather than those things that larger churches are known for such as worship experience. Perhaps that which someone feels they need to bring will add little value to what actually energizes your church at this point and time.

Needers also come in a second flavor. Those are the people who love to tell you how much they need you. They will say things like, "I am so looking forward to being able to call up my pastor whenever I need him." They also might say, "I was so busy at my last church. It will be great to breathe for a while!"

Whether you encounter runners or needers, do not be afraid to get honest with them. The challenge of faithfully trusting God for the right people now can prevent a litany of headaches from the wrong people later on. Now, don't get all mean-spirited about it. You don't need to bludgeon them with fancy church planting terminology or paint yourself as the more spiritual person. Simply paint a picture of the reality of what will be expected of them with the emphasis on your expectations, not theirs. Brutal, I know.

The third key tactic I have employed in order to stretch in my faithfulness to what Christ desired to build in his church is simply viewing each person as a member of the kingdom first, before they are a member of my church. Simply put, every believer belongs in a church, but not every

3. McIntosh, *Taking Your Church to the Next Level*, 136.

believer belongs in your church. Obviously, you want your church to be a place of mission, ministry, and family for as many as possible, but do not drain yourself or depress yourself with the belief that you need to "win" every single person to your church. It's not your church.

Faithfully adhering to this belief takes so much pressure off of the expectations you put on yourself. God is responsible for the direction of each and every believer and you're not him. To lighten the moment, here is a newsflash: Not everyone attending the church down the street is where they should be either. Faithfully trust God for filling in the spaces with kingdom pieces as he sees fit. Life is easier that way and more enjoyable.

I know that exhibiting faithfulness both in you and your church body seems a bit random, but don't allow that to keep you from prioritizing the metric. The faithful planter looks at Christ and prays daily that he might build his church. The faithful planter then trusts in the results of that prayer, despite the pressure from elsewhere to be something other. Walk in faith and do it boldly.

4

The Extraordinary Message

Rooted in Donuts

THERE IS A CHURCH that I am familiar with that grew out of donuts. I remember seeing the press clippings when the church first started, and the pastor was in a photograph on the front cover of the Sunday newspaper taking boxes of donuts outside and giving them to all who passed by and came inside. The picture grabbed my attention to say the least. I dove into the article to see how a church could grow out of glazed and chocolate-iced deliciousness. I was not a church planter quite yet, God was still working on my heart at that time, but I admired anyone who could grow a church.

On and off through the years our family had opportunity to visit that church while on vacation. I remember being excited the first time I went because I was now a church planter and I wanted to see behind the curtain and get a glimpse at what makes a church so big and appealing. I also was ready to enjoy some time of personal refreshing under the teaching of another pastor.

The first time I went I remember feeling encouraged by how friendly everyone was, from the parking lot straight to our seat in the auditorium. Certainly, this was a strength and a key reason for their success. I even grabbed a donut (ok, maybe two) in the lobby. My family found the music to be refreshing. It wasn't overly polished but certainly authentic and worshipful. The pastor even jumped in on some of the songs. The church was two for two in my book.

Granted, one of the hardest things for a pastor to do is visit another church and not get caught up in comparisons and judgments. I actually work very hard to appreciate each and every evangelical church for its own unique vision and personality. What happened next on that first Sunday visit led me to a bit of donut heartburn.

When the time came for the pastor to get up and deliver his sermon, we were all greeted with a lot of pictures from his recent vacation and whimsical stories of his hiking foibles. He declared the beauty of God's creation and threw in a scripture verse or two. After several reprisals of, "Can I get an amen!?", he asked for the distribution of the offering baskets. I was heartsick. I heard zero mention of the gospel and practically zero mention of Jesus. No one was confronted with the reality of sin. No one was challenged to reflect on the Savior. No one was given hope in personal forgiveness from a loving God.

About a year later we were on vacation once again and we had family now attending the same church. They invited us to spend our Sunday with them and not wanting to throw an entire ministry out the window from one observation I cheerfully agreed. Everything was the same in that we were greeted warmly, the music touched our hearts, and the pastor preached a sermon with practically zero biblical content. The donuts had more sustenance. When the opportunity came to go back a third time we decided to attend elsewhere. The church had grown around some wonderful qualities but was lacking one of the basic, most essential qualities leading to a failing metric.

Rooted in the Message

Perhaps, like me, you are convinced that you are unqualified in one or more ways to fulfill the calling the God has placed upon your life. Maybe you have always lacked any kind of organization skill. Your teenagers room looks tidier than what is going on in your head most of the time. Maybe you have to work really hard at personal evangelism. Maybe you have never been a real "out front" kind of person like me. Nothing about me wishes to have any portion of limelight. I would much rather be in the corner somewhere with a book in my hand than be surround by or in front of any sizeable group of people. I have even been known to struggle with the responsibility of being the "final word" on just about anything. If it wasn't that I have some sense of spiritual responsibility, I would probably tell my children to "go ask your mother" in just about every circumstance. Yet here we are, church planters, prospective planters, or even team members, looking to leverage everything that we are not, for a cause that is so big that it scares us to death.

So, what holds us together? What should motivate us to reach beyond who we are not to a purpose higher than ourselves. I believe it is the simple fact that whatever I do, it is not about me. Early on in my vocational ministry years, I used to really get hung-up on the areas where I felt like I was inadequate or unqualified. It was during one of these episodes that our Lord gave me a life verse in 1 Cor 2:1–5:

> And I, when I came to you, brothers, did not come proclaiming to you the testimony of God with lofty speech or wisdom. For I decided to know nothing among you except Jesus Christ and him crucified. And I was with you in weakness and in fear and much trembling, and my speech and my message were not in plausible words of wisdom, but in demonstration of the Spirit and of power, so that your faith might not rest in the wisdom of men but in the power of God.

There is so much "razzle-dazzle" going on in the world today, one might think that creativity, marketing acumen and entrepreneurship would be all that is required to make a great church start and eventually a great church. Many church planters wrestle with not being witty enough, polished enough, handsome enough, and relevant enough. I understand the need for some sort of relevance. You can't speak to a generation and culture that you do not know and cannot relate to. With that said, at the rate of change that our culture is undergoing today, just trying to remain relevant would probably require multiple staff members at launch dedicated to just that one task.

To illustrate the challenge of trying to remain culturally relevant I submit the issue of gay marriage. In his thought-provoking book, *We Cannot Be Silent,* Albert Mohler cites the quick change in the cultural attitude toward same-sex marriage. Polling showed that as recently as 2008 a vast majority of Americans were still ready to label homosexual behavior as immoral and stood against the legalization of same-sex marriage. Within six years polls showed a massive shift on this topic with the majority of Americans in favor of gay marriage and an even larger majority showing that they had no negative moral judgments on homosexuality or same-sex relationships.[1] People are fickle in opinion and, if you'll excuse my alliteration, people are

---

1. Mohler, *We Cannot Be Silent,* 34.

getting fickle, faster. Trying to appeal to emotion, culture or opinion is hard and only going to get more difficult. One day you're cool if your church has an industrial background and the next day you're outdated because shiplap has taken over the church planting world. If you are reading this and don't know what shiplap is, I thank you for illustrating my point.

A popular trend among churches right now is to use the "At the Movies" sermon series once a year. During the series, money is invested in movie sets in the lobby, costumes for staff members and extended movie clips to drive sermon delivery. Obviously the trend will have its fans and its detractors, with detractors lamenting the amount of time spent in Hollywood verses the word of God.

Wherever you fall on the spectrum of relevance, allow me to offer up the words of John Wesley: "God Himself has condescended to teach the way; for this very end He came from heaven. He hath written it down in a book. O give me that book! At any price, give me the book of God!"[2] If you are going to be known for something as a planter and as a church, may it be the gospel of Christ. May everything you do serve the high purpose of getting God's word into those who encounter your ministry. May they not hear your wisdom or fall for your bait and switch, but rather, may they hear the very word of God brought down to their own ears.

God's word can do what your words cannot. God's word can do what no motivational speaker or skilled communicator can do. God's word can rip open a person's life and point the divine finger of truth right to their very soul. The writer of Hebrews boldly proclaims this work of God's word stating, "For the word of God is living and active, sharper than any two-edged sword, piercing to the division of soul and of spirit, of joints and of marrow, and discerning the thoughts and intentions of the heart." (Heb 4:12) They may love your vacation slides, but they need the truth of God's word and the message of the cross.

Church Planting Metric Four: Gospel-Centered

Several years ago, I had the enormous privilege to be able to personally invite three men to join me as I led a training program for those exhibiting signs of potential ministry leadership. It was a fairly simplistic program I developed myself based on some of the best writings and practices of men that I respected and learned from. We read, studied and discussed

2. Wesley, *Preface to Standard Sermons*, lines 15–16.

from great names like Henry Blackaby, John MacArthur, Gene Wilkes, and Charles Spurgeon to name a few. These three men became the highlight of my ministry life as we met together once a month after spending the previous thirty days pouring over the reading assignments, while fulfilling their homework assignments that we would later critique and discuss as a group.

The curriculum was loosely devised around the three C's of spiritual leaders: calling, character and competencies. When we got to competencies, each man was given an opportunity to study, prepare, and share a fifteen-minute sermon on a passage of scripture that I chose ahead of time. They all did an admirable job for their first time preaching, yet only one excelled in the hidden criteria. Only one wove the gospel into their text and shared it from the pulpit. Afterward we all complemented him and when I asked him if he wove in the gospel deliberately, he paid me one of the highest compliments that I have ever received. He told me that he has always admired my preaching because I always highlighted the gospel from any text and shared how a person can be saved in Christ. He thought that he should do the same.

It should not be lost on us that Jesus Christ is called the Word of God in the prologue of John's gospel account. We quickly learn that he is the eternal word, existent from the very beginning (John 1:1) and that later that same Word put on flesh and walked among us. (John 1:14) This is significant because it reminds each and every believer from the back row Baptist to the fiery preacher in the pulpit that the Bible has always been the story of Jesus, from Genesis through the Gospels and until the triumphant return. Jesus existed before the world. (John 1:1) Jesus created the world. (John 1:3) The scriptures point us toward our sin and toward our need for him. The Old Testament holds up a mirror to our pride, our stubbornness, our legalism, and our idolatry among so many other things. The Old Testament leaves us panting for someone to save us. I love Job's cry in Job 9:32–35:

> For he is not a man, as I am, that I might answer him, that we should come to trial together. There is no arbiter between us, who might lay his hand on us both. Let him take his rod away from me, and let not dread of him terrify me. Then I would speak without fear of him, for I am not so in myself.

We arrive at the gospels with a palpable anticipation of God's deliverance.

This is to be the overarching narrative of your message, the gospel of Jesus Christ. You will be encouraged by other denominational or ministry veterans to spend many of your preaching days focused on topical or cultural messages such as Veterans Day, Father's Day, "Pro-life Sunday", or maybe even "Get Out the Vote Sunday". Whatever you preach, may it always bring folks back to their need for a wonderful savior. Here are three practical reasons why this is so important. One, your church is typically going to have a least one person sitting in a pew or seat each Sunday who has not responded to the gospel. Two, most people in your church are not comfortable sharing the gospel and/or they are not exercising the energy or faith to do it. By hearing the stories and reality of man's lostness each week, it creates an urgency in many of your folks. Three, self-help and social justice have become the loudest voice in the evangelical room right now and these two topics are like a gigantic black hole sucking out every other message of greater importance. Paul understood the urgency with each passing opportunity to communicate before other men and women. He said, "For necessity is laid upon me. Woe to me if I do not preach the gospel!" (1 Cor 9:16) Paul said that, not Tony Robbins.

Gospel-Centered Means Everybody, Everywhere

If you are anything like me, social media is something like a love/hate relationship. Every time I want to delete my account or throw my smartphone into the Gulf of Mexico, I come across something that makes me smile or laugh. You love those cat videos because they make you chuckle as you sit in the school pick-up line. You treasure those pictures of your friends' children as they grow up and prosper. You even laugh a bit and hold the phone up to your spouse to show her the funniest meme about marital flatulence.

However, after scrolling through forty-five minutes of mindless posts rather than listening to your daughter's orchestra concert you observe the darker side of social media. It may be a pastor that you know from another part of the country who posts about how his four-year-old just memorized the first chapter of James before being tucked into bed that night. They inform you in their post that "little Jeremiah is going to change the world for Jesus someday". You however, are still trying to get your nine-year-old to rinse the toothpaste out of the sink before bed.

But the bigger knife to a pastor's heart on social media is often your own church members. There used to be a sweet era of blissful ignorance when all that you knew about the Jones family was that they lived in a nice home, loved their kids and showed up to church most Sundays. Now you know that Tim Jones replies to all his fantasy football buddies trash talk with "unwholesome" words. You learn that Tim's wife, Rita Jones, posts more duck-face selfies in public restrooms than you can handle. You even learn that postage stamps cover more than little Abbie Jones' homecoming dress.

All of these analogies are either true to me or another pastor I know. I remember sharing a sermon one Sunday morning and a nice young woman I had known for a while came up to me and complimented me on what she called a "truly eye opening and convicting message". I thanked her and began to wonder if God was doing a work in her life. She had shared her testimony of salvation with me a long time ago but always seemed to operate on the fringe. I went home that afternoon encouraged and prompted to pray for her.

The next day, I found myself on social media scrolling through status updates. Here was this same young woman posting about how her horoscope from that morning had been "spot-on". She was certain that her horoscope was never going to let her down. I now had a member of my church, a baptized believer of my church, posting on social media how her guiding truth was astrology, printed each morning in the paper. Insert face-palm emoji here.

My fear is that the "easy believism" of the church growth movement has led us to a place of lifestyle messages reflecting something other than the gospel. The person's backside in the seat on Sunday is looking more like a person's backslide on Monday. The gospel means the message of good news through every delivery method possible…especially our day to day lives. The disconnect between what the Bible teaches and what every day Christians are preaching is growing at an alarming rate. Now, please understand that I'm not advocating some works-based or legalistic religion. I'm just suggesting that the message of the gospel in your church should extend beyond the pulpit on Sunday. I'm suggesting that there should be a way for what we communicate through our sermon to be the sermon lived out the rest of the week. I believe that this is what Paul was emphasizing when he said in Phil 2:12–13, "Therefore, my beloved, as you have always obeyed, so now, not only as in my presence but much more in my absence, work out your own salvation with fear and trembling, for it is God who works in you, both to will and to work for his good pleasure." More posts of scripture, more offers to help others, more kind uplifting posts, and less horoscopes and prosperity gospel quotes. And maybe a few more cat videos.

Getting Beyond Horoscopes

It seems like the mountain of cultural obstacles demanding the ear and the attention of your folks is growing at an astronomical rate. If it's not social media, it's youth sports, boating, travel, podcasts, online church or worldwide pandemics. Most of it is enough to make any church planter feel defeated before they ever really begin.

Yet Paul clearly admonishes us to not give up when the deck seems stacked against us. His solution seems pretty simple in 2 Tim 4:1–4:

> I charge you in the presence of God and of Christ Jesus, who is to judge the living and the dead, and by his appearing and his kingdom: preach the word; be ready in season and out of season; reprove, rebuke, and exhort, with complete patience and teaching. For the time is coming when people will not endure sound teaching, but having itching ears they will accumulate for themselves teachers to suit their own passions, and will turn away from listening to the truth and wander off into myths.

I think it is safe to say that as planters, churches and pastors, we are out of season. I also think it is safe to say that our modern culture has developed a huge segment of society, even within the church, who will not endure sound teaching. Yet Paul's solution to this, as he encouraged the young pastor/planter Timothy, is "preach the word".

One of your great challenges as a church planter is going to be your willingness to stand against culture and preach truth when you know that truth will not result in a fast-growing church. You may ask, "How can I do this when my church plant is an exaggerated mix of mature believers as well as the lost or the highly immature unchurched?" It might appear a lot easier for the pastor down the street at the larger established church to preach truth to a congregation of 500 regular attending believers than for you and your fledgling church of forty. Most who don't know the difference between a tithe and a trick, or an Apostle and an epistle.

I've found through the years that one of the more proven methods for me has been to focus on what I see as three timeless truths: relate, exposit and apply. These three are by no means meant to replace a good hermeneutic or perhaps what you were taught in a good hermeneutics class. These three simply keep me honest as I attempt to share God's word with those from all walks of the cultural and religious spectrum.

Relate

Why would you expect anyone to listen to what you have to say if they are unable to relate? In all of your time spent in preparation and study this might be the one area that causes the most consternation and demands the most time. When Jesus would preach or teach to large crowds, small crowds or groups of individuals he would often start out with a parable, a question, or he might simply say, "You have heard it said…". Each tool worked to draw the listener in based upon something that they could relate to. Relating may involve taking off your shoes and putting on another's shoes for five precious minutes. It also may involve finding a pair of flip flops that fit everyone in the room so that they fix their gaze and their eyes on you for what's about to come.

The early days of Covid taught us a lot of things about ourselves. It taught us that as American families we can survive being locked up in the same house for extended periods of time without requiring body bags. It showed us that food delivery services are like the cockroaches of an economic disaster. While just about every other business was constricting, laying off or, sadly, going out of business due to lockdowns, the food delivery service expanded. No longer was Door Dash simply for the Millennial living on your basement couch. Now everyone noticed its merits and began downloading their apps.

If we begin asking questions about the human condition based around the scriptures, we will find that, much like Covid lockdowns, we have plenty in common and much that we all can relate to. It is possible to draw in listeners from all kinds of varied backgrounds as you then lead them to the truth of God's word. Jesus showed us that this doesn't need to be a long and drawn out process. A simple question like, "How many in the room have struggled to keep a diet?" can be just as effective as a story about the time you responded to the wrong person in a text message and almost lost a friendship.

Exposit

Expository preaching always begins with what the Bible has to say and teaching that to the hearer. You may come at it from a verse-by-verse approach or more of a topical approach. Either way, it is better because it details what God says rather than what you, or someone else, thinks.

Many good things beg for the time of a church planter. In any given week I'm regularly volunteering somewhere so that I can meet people (preferably lost people). I spend time each morning in prayer for my family, my church and those things that are a concern to either me or those people that I care about. I handle administrative functions for our church such as creating and copying worship guides, creating media for Sunday mornings, visiting the post office box or maybe even scrubbing a toilet or two. I call, email or visit church family. I lead small groups. I take time to plan for the future whether it be budgets, outreach projects or community engagement. Yes, I even work on the dreaded reports for my denomination. Yet, while many good things will beg for the time of a church planter, perhaps the most sacred is studying God's word for proclamation to each and every audience you have.

I have learned that typically, expositional verse-by-verse preaching is most effective for me and keeps me honest in my approach to sharing. It's not me placing my ideas upon scripture but, rather, the other way around. Plus, when you preach verse-by-verse, it is more difficult to shy away from the difficult passages. In my experience, when folks see a verse coming and they know it is hard, they appreciate you tackling it and often lean in even closer.

Apply

I may have mentioned that I'm a bit of a space geek. Back in February of 2018, many, including myself, witnessed Space X launch the first test flight of their Falcon Heavy rocket. The purpose behind its design is to carry heavy cargo such as satellites and sections for the space station as well as launches that would explore deeper into space. To the delight of many at Space X and those watching abroad, when Falcon Heavy got ready to break earths orbital bonds the cargo was revealed. In the capsule was a Tesla which belonged to the owner of Space X, Elon Musk. Inside the pretty red roadster was "Starman". A mannequin dressed in a space suit listening to an endless loop of Space Oddity by David Bowie. You can actually track Starman online if you want to know where he's at, where he's headed and how fast. To me this is a wonderful example of application. Starman was helping to open many of our eyes to the ability to put ourselves in a Space X rocket and take a ride in space. Maybe you can't afford the ride. I'm a church planter so I know I can't. But some have already signed up.

Biblical application is really the difference between preaching for the purpose of knowledge verses preaching for life change. Jeff Christopherson put it this way, "The Bible was never given to us for our information but for our transformation. There must be an application of spiritual truths in order to see a transformation in our spiritual lives."[3] Most who know me really well will tell you that nothing gets me going more than to see a person "get" God's word and then turn around and apply it in their lives in such a way as they experience godly change. And before you think that doesn't apply to a church planter because they are small or have more important things to worry about, I want you to know that I have seen some amazing life-change stories occur out of little church plants. I have witnessed individuals surrender to Christ, surrender to ministry, forgive adulteress spouses, restore marriages, and forgive sworn enemies. Believe it or not I have even observed people volunteer to serve in children's ministry!

The message that your church plant carries is more extraordinary than anyone could possibly imagine. The tyranny of the urgent speaks to us all and in a loud voice demands of our attention and affection. The tyranny of the urgent says that this cultural demand or that denominational demand is the latest and greatest thing to grow your church. The easy road also vies for our attention and leads us to take short cuts as we share, preach and teach. The Deceiver would love nothing more than for you to plant a church rooted in good stories, personal charisma and weekly photos of your pets or your vacation. I challenge you to stand firmly in God's word and get it in front of and into your people, both the lost and the saved.

3. Christopherson, *Kingdom First,* 125.

5

The Extraordinary Mission

Last Call

My long-time good friend, Dean, is a funeral director. In my opinion he is one of the best at his job. He works incredibly hard to put people at ease during one of life's most difficult times. He weaves compassion, wit, humor and an easy-going demeanor to supplement a family's time of grief with joy and remembrance. On occasion, a family will meet with Dean to arrange for the care of a deceased loved one and in the course of conversation they will share with him that they do not have a minister. This is not uncommon, especially in places like southern Florida after migrating from other parts of the country. Dean is very kingdom minded and asks them if they would prefer to have a Christian pastor. If they do, then he will often recommend me because he knows my heart.

Dean and I have many memories working together to provide care for families in need. These are memories that extend back almost twenty years. We have stood in many cemeteries together including several national cemeteries where we memorialized and buried America's service men and women. We have grieved together during services for families and friends that we knew well. We have stood over caskets for accident victims, cancer victims, mommies and daddies, and the littlest of children. However, one of our most interesting funerals began with an unusual phone call.

Approximately fifteen years ago Dean called me to ask if I was available to help a client in need of a Christian pastor to perform the memorial service. Before I could answer, he told me, "There are a couple of interesting notes regarding this service, Larry." Intrigued, I asked him to explain. He said that the loved one making the arrangements was the long-time girlfriend of the deceased and that her boyfriend was an avid motorcycle rider. The request was for the funeral to be held in a local biker bar in town. Wondering when I might have another opportunity to share Christ in a biker bar, I told Dean to sign me up.

I called the girlfriend and told her that I had never officiated a funeral in a biker bar before. Knowing the general clientele, I asked her if her boyfriend would prefer me to dress casual or wear a suit. She began to cry over the phone and quietly asked, "Would you mind wearing a suit?" I knew I was on to something.

When Dean and I arrived, I got out of my truck and put on my suit coat and began to weave in between some pretty amazing Harley's in the parking lot, dodging clouds of cigarette smoke, smiling and nodding to everyone I saw. Once inside we were pleasantly surprised to see that they attempted to cover up most of the pictures of semi-nude women on the walls and had placed a small stage in the front. The bartender came up to me and informed me that when I was done, he wanted to ring his bell, and hoist a shot for "one last call" to Rick. He stared me in the eye and said, "That won't be a problem for you, will it?" Perhaps out of an instinct of self-preservation, my immediate response was, "Nope, not at all, sir." I could see Dean smirking out of the corner of my eye.

They played a couple country songs and then it was my turn. I stood up on the small stage in the middle of that smokey bar and spoke about love and why relationships matter. I shared about the greatest relationship of all, a Savior who chose sinners and tax collectors over the religious elite. I shared the need to be saved in Jesus. I offered a prayer of salvation and in my heart asked that God might deliver someone. I wish I could tell you the story ended with a mass revival of bikers in Sarasota, Florida, but it did not. I do know this, Rick's girlfriend cried and hugged me and told me that if all pastors were as approachable as me she probably would have tried going to church. That day I truly felt like a missionary. A genuine laborer in the harvest.

Living Missional

Why would I wax on with this story? Because I love telling it? That's true. Because I cherish the memory? That's true as well. But mostly because I believe it is important for each and every church planter and pastor to always consider missional living as a priority in their lives. And if it is a priority in your life, it will be a priority in the life of your church plant.

At its very essence, the mission is simple. As humans we've managed to make it in to many things, but Jesus put it simply this way in Matt 28:19–20: "Go therefore and make disciples of all nations, baptizing them in the name of the Father and of the Son and of the Holy Spirit, teaching them to observe all that I have commanded you. And behold, I am with you always, to the end of the age." Sir Isaac Newton taught us a lot of things among which is the fact that everything has a gravitational pull. The bigger the mass of a body, the larger it's gravitational pull will be. I think Jesus understood that our tendency as humans would be to gravitate towards that which is biggest in our life. We gravitate towards family. We gravitate towards stadiums. We gravitate towards careers. We are never going to naturally gravitate towards lost neighbors, strangers and communities. Therefore, Jesus started the Great Commission with "go". Living an outward focused life is going to mean pushing back against that which easily draws us in, so as to reach more in the areas that may make us uncomfortable.

Planter, as you develop a core team and eventually launch a service you will have some sort of church. That church will be important to you and like a gravitational pull, you will feel drawn (obligated) to minister to it. That's not wrong. Just do not allow it to keep you from going to the less comfortable, less important places and spaces to continue to touch lost lives. I don't know what your biker bar might be, maybe a bowling alley, a political club, or a Jewish neighbor. Just make sure you go. Live outwardly focused so that those in your church will be compelled to do likewise.

Church Planting Metric Five: Relationship Building

Much like watching grass grow, developing a missional mindset and culture in your church plant will take time and maybe even develop some weeds along the way. I would love to be able to tell you that in my first church plant as well as my current church plant, the message of missional living took off like wildfire, but that would be an extreme exaggeration. Calling it merely an exaggeration might be a bit of an exaggeration as well. My constant drumbeat in sermons, small groups, core groups and training is always the same. I remind each and every person that God has blessed them with a unique circle of influence, putting them in the key position to speak gospel truth into the lives of others. I always ask my folks to consider and pray about their unique circle of influence.

There is not one single person in your church who is exempt from the work of the Great Commission, from the pastor right down to the introvert who only cares about running sound and media. You know that person. They get more excited about the latest update to the media software or the functionality of the church media on the website than just about anything else. They run up to you almost panting with excitement and say things like, "Pastor, pastor! We can now do a picture-in-picture instant twitter poll during your sermon!" You scratch your head and simply wonder if he or she heard one word of the sermon you just labored over and delivered. You pray that they still see every aspect of their life as a reflection of the Great Commission.

Each person has a vital circle of gospel influence. A church that begins to live this way, despite the numeric results, is light years ahead of many churches in America today. Dustin Willis and Aaron Coe put it this way:

> the mission of God requires that believers leverage their lives for His glory. The Great Commission is not for a select few, it is for the entirety of the church. The movement of God's mission sweeps across everyday, ordinary lives to draw in businesspeople, soccer moms, grandmothers, neighbors, students, lawyers, teachers, baristas, contractors, white collar, blue collar, or no collar at all.[1]

When the saints in your church core team or church body begin to see their lives as a significant key to getting Jesus into the lives of those in their circle of influence, you have achieved a significant metric.

Nancy and Rachel were professors at a Christian college in central Pennsylvania. Nancy was on the latter side of her career with books and awards to her credit. Rachel was a brand new PhD, brand new to central Pennsylvania and brand new to our church. Yet both women had one thing in common beyond their employer. They saw their lives as missionaries to college students.

Both women were leaders in our fledgling church, yet the professors took it upon themselves to reach out to their students with the gospel and

---

1. Willis and Coe, *Life on Mission*, 25.

to invite them to join in our gospel fellowship. We were a church that was not surrounded by any college or university of significant size, yet because of the heart and mindset of these women we were always fellowshipping with college students, engaging them with scripture, and we were blessed to even start a class for just college and career aged adults. I've had the privilege to see some of these students come to Christ, to go on to serve the Lord and to even perform wedding ceremonies for some. It is a ministry that I could never have orchestrated on my own at the genesis of our plant, yet because two professors were thinking missionally, God did some great work out of their circle of influence! And thanks to social media, I can still see the work that some of these students (now adults) are performing for Christ. And for the record, God did this in a church that never grew above 125 in attendance.

I Become

The Apostle Paul had a very focused view of gospel living that could best be described as "missional". He understood the importance of developing intimate relationships for the purpose of sharing Christ. In 1 Cor 9:19–23 he said these incredibly important words:

> For though I am free from all, I have made myself a servant to all, that I might win more of them. To the Jews I became as a Jew, in order to win Jews. To those under the law I became as one under the law (though not being myself under the law) that I might win those under the law. To those outside the law I became as one outside the law (not being outside the law of God but under the law of Christ) that I might win those outside the law. To the weak I became weak, that I might win the weak. I have become all things to all people, that by all means I might save some. I do it all for the sake of the gospel, that I may share with them in its blessings.

Missional living means viewing one's life through the lens of intentional relationships. You practice exercising relational engagement knowing that you may be the only gospel that someone else may hear and you go about it with a sacrificial attitude. Willis and Coe state it this way, "Life on mission is about intersecting gospel intentionality into our everyday routines."[2] I love the phrase "gospel intentionality" because it reflects what I see as a kingdom mindset. It reflects Paul's heart of "I become". I also love

2. Willis and Coe, *Life on Mission*, 27.

that phrase, "everyday routines". This means that the everyday person is created to be an extraordinary missionary.

I enjoy telling those in my church that they are not merely a lawyer or a grandmother. They are a missionary, cleverly disguised as a lawyer or grandmother. This is important because you probably already have a sense for the way most people in your church plant see their daily lives. Their job is to survive. Someone is threatening their position at work and they just want to survive. A new young person moved into the office next to them and they are just trying to survive their politics and "know it all" attitude. A senior adult is off to their third appointment with a doctor this week and they just want to survive. A healthy church is the church that sees their lives as opportunities to not simply survive, but to form relationships for the purpose of missional engagement. This is hard, but it begins when we become all people to foster an intersectionality of the gospel and our everyday lives.

Take It From Patrick of Ireland

It is pure joy for me to see and hear the creative ways in which church planters labor so hard and so specifically to reach their communities. I've never met a guy trying to plant a church who said that they were coasting along because they felt that church planting was the easiest route to retirement. If I'm being honest, very little about my regular income bothers me while church planting. What keeps me awake at night is my vapid ability to trust God with my latter years. However, I remind myself that God is good and I'm not planting for a 401(k). Neither are most planters that I know.

My friend, John, is a great example of working really hard to enable engagement of a culture that is hurtling toward post-Christianity. John planted and now pastors a church in Harrisburg, the state capital of Pennsylvania. My young church had opportunity to help John's church and serve his core group as they got started. His church has transitioned through the years from a semi-suburban church to an intentional urban church. One constant through all the years of their church has been the struggle to engage people personally and missionally. That's when the leadership of his church met and began to joke about all the crazy reasons why the people they meet don't want to go to church. The negative reasons became an absolutely crazy idea to reach more in their community.

So about four years into their story, his church launched a campaign to tell their community to "don't go to church". Throughout neighborhoods and at intersections, yard signs began to pop up that said, "Don't Go to Church!" and simply listed a website address. The website took curious neighbors to a series of videos from church leadership detailing multiple reasons to not go to church. I marveled at the creativity of John's leadership. He told me later, "As we joked about those things, we realized they'd actually be reasons others WOULD want to come to our church." You might go to a video that detailed the fact that you'll find former prisoners at their church. Former prisoners, like all sinners, are welcome at their church because church is not designed for perfect people. If you were looking for a church full of perfect people, then "don't go". John told me that they had many mixed reactions to their campaign, many hits on their videos, healthy conversations about the purpose of the church and the gospel and even some new faces who came as a result.

In an urban environment with one of the highest homicide rates per capita in the nation, John was using the acceptance of former prisoners to their church as a way to speak life into his community. This is part of what George Hunter would call "The Celtic Way of Evangelism". Hunter's book by the same name is an encouraging tool for planters seeking to once again claim the west for Christ. Though not written specifically for planters, it lays out much like a guidebook for engaging people through missional communities. Hunter begins, as most planters should, with the reality that the days of traditional western church engagement are passing us by. He bluntly states, "In the face of this changing Western culture, many Western Church leaders are in denial; they plan and do church as though next year will be 1957."[3] Ouch! This is why I love listening to my friend, John, and all church planters because they may not be church growth experts, or masters of administering large Sunday School programs, but they are not planning in the 1950's. They may be a little crazy, and their churches may be a little small compared to traditional models of years gone by, but they are thinking differently.

If I'm a betting man (I'm Baptist, so of course I'm not) I would guess that most church planters are not investing heavily in choir robes, bait-and-switch giveaways, massive five or six figure Easter Passion Plays and my favorite, Singing Christmas Trees. Most church planters are trying to move their churches to meet the next generation where they are at through

---

3. Hunter, *The Celtic Way of Evangelism*, 9.

personal relationships, conversations and diagnosing community need. Be encouraged, because this takes time, some trial and error, and a church that buys into missional community.

Hunter details the success of Patrick of Ireland returning to the island where he was once held captive in order to set the heathen spiritual captives free in Christ. Patrick would take a dozen or more Christians including priests, seminarians and some women and set up a camp of faith adjacent to a heathen tribal settlement. Then the "apostolic team would meet the people, engage them in conversation and in ministry and look for people who appeared receptive." They would pray for them and serve them through arts, storytelling, or even drama. Patrick would receive the people's questions and answer accordingly.[4]

The goal was church planting. This ancient process of engaging the community would often takes months and if it proved successful, they would start a church adjacent to the tribe that would look remarkably indigenous.[5] I love this model, probably because it is much less formulaic, way more personal and definitely not what you are going to hear at the latest costly planter conference run by megachurches with handsome speakers and a profound worship experience.

Be free, planter, from the chains of always having to regurgitate another massive successful event that can only be pulled off when mission teams from some other large church outside your community wants to send their youth to help. I love those churches and those youth groups and certainly appreciate some of the publicity that you can get, but don't allow it to shape your philosophy of personal engagement. Perhaps you spend time in prayer with your team simply asking for God to reveal connection points to those in your community. Maybe your town is steeped in history and it is a point of great pride within the community. Several from within your team decide to serve on the board of the historical preservation society or they begin volunteering as researchers. Maybe, like my crazy friend, John, your church embraces your urban community for the struggles that it continually endures and strives to engage in a conversation that leads to freedom. Look like your community. Talk to your community. Love your community. Don't feel the need to be the church from 1957 (or even 1989) in someone else's community.

4. Hunter, *The Celtic Way of Evangelism*, 21.
5. Hunter, *The Celtic Way of Evangelism*, 22.

Church Planting Metric Six: Making Disciples

People are messy. Let me amend that statement . . . people are really messy. Even the ones who have it all put together on the outside. There is an awesome scene in the 2005 movie, "Hitch" where Will Smith's character tries to impress a hard-nosed, highly successful, cynical female tabloid journalist on their first date. Hitch is known for having all the right moves and the ability to woo a woman no matter what. Hitch decides to impress on the first date by going jet-skiing to Ellis Island and then locating the actual records of this young woman's immigrant family. Expecting the best, one of the park rangers points to a line in one of the actual books used to process immigrants into the United States. Hitch's expectation of success is through the moon at this point. He is planning on racking up major brownie points with his date. But things don't go quite like he planned.

His date, Sara, slowly begins to recognize the signature in the book as her great-great-grandfather. As she begins to become emotional, Hitch senses that he has done well. But Sara's emotions quickly turn to screaming, obvious emotional pain, and she runs away. Hitch says to the ranger, "I saw that going differently in my mind." Sara later explains to Hitch that she became so angry because her great-great-grandfather was actually a well-known murderer in his hometown overseas. Having that in her past has always been a little haunting. Seeing his signature in print made it all too real for her.

People come in all shapes and sizes. Some wear their heart on their sleeve while others will always look polished and content on the outside. Yet one thing is for certain, deep down in the life of each and every person is some sort of mess. It may be their present, it may be their past. It may be their choices, it may be their personality, or it may even be their personal hygiene. So messy are people and the strange tangle that they leave that my wife is convinced that it is one of the core reasons why true discipleship in the American church is not happening today.

It's almost like a pastime for me to watch my wife try and set up a time to disciple three college-aged women. In order to set up coffee and discussion around their growth in Christ she feels like she has to climb K2. Three young women who cancel more than they meet. Three young women who somehow put off the vibe that they need nineteen different calendars to keep up with their very busy lives. Three young women, who think that my Mindy couldn't possibly understand how busy they are. Three young women who oversleep because life is hard and tiring. This spiritual business with these girls is messy. This is discipleship. My wife never gives up, she just keeps calling and texting and praying and eventually she gets to pour into their lives. I think she does this because when she was nineteen, another young married woman in Auburn, Alabama put up with the messiness of my wife and her roommates ad nauseum so that she could pour her life into them. Messy is a given. Sadly in today's churches, making disciples is not.

I'm not a trained missiologist, I don't have a popular blog for deep thinkers and I've never led a study of any kind. But, with enough Diet Coke and time to myself, I can sometimes formulate some educated guesses just by connecting cultural dots. I'm often left wondering if one of the hangovers from the church growth movement is a high percentage of churches with great attendance and few committed disciples.

This train of thought is what drew me to Kyle Idleman's book, *Not a Fan*. If you haven't read it, be warned, conviction will follow. Kyle speaks to what I believe to be at the heart of churches and genuine disciples. We've raised generations of Jesus fans, but few followers. He shares in his book:

> Many have made a decision to believe in Jesus without making a commitment to follow Jesus. The gospel allows for no such distinction. Biblical belief is more than mental assent or verbal acknowledgment. Many fans have repeated a prayer or raised their hand or walked forward at the end of a sermon and made a decision to believe, but there was never a commitment to follow. Jesus never offered such an option.[6]

Ouch! Even though the church is not the subject of his statement, the indictment is pretty clear. Churches have made a lot of converts that might show up on Monday morning reports, but have churches made followers or genuine disciples?

What's at the End of the Aisle?

This particular issue might resonate more with me because I have felt the confusion set before me as a fledgling Christian. I trusted in Christ, was born again and baptized as a teenager. A few years later I started to make my way into certain churches that really wanted to see that walk down the aisle. I listened as they pushed for that hand and that step out into the aisle while everyone else's "head was bowed and eyes were closed". You know the

---

6. Idleman, *Not a Fan*, 32.

drill. I began to wonder if I was really saved because I had never walked an aisle. I even scheduled a time to speak with a visiting pastor one Sunday evening after a revival meeting. He kept pressuring me to get saved, but I believed that I already was. I just wanted to know why others had to walk an aisle.

Now don't get angry at me about the aisle thing. I'm sure there are pastors reading this and they will defend to the death the fact that the aisle merely represents a commitment. As a middle-aged pastor myself who struggled through the confusion of that "commitment", I'm merely asking, "Is it?". I too have given invitations and asked people to come forward. I wanted to pray with them, get to know them, connect them with a counselor. I don't really do that anymore. I ask them to tell me after the service and to tell the person who invited them. I believe that connecting them with the person who is most invested in them is the best first step in making followers rather than fans.

Please don't hear me say that every church needs to give up their decision time at the end of the service that involves a stroll down the aisle. I'm more asking, what's the purpose and what's waiting at the end of the aisle? To be honest, like many other church planters reading this, the walk down the aisle was never much of a problem for me anyway because rarely did my church plants meet in a space with much of an aisle.

My fear is that too many churches, including church plants as well as church planters are hoping that they are making disciples rather than practicing some type of intentionality to see it through. Coe and Willis bolster this idea by stating, that "we cannot simply hope disciple-making into existence. We cannot put a sign on our church property that says, 'Now Making Disciples! Join us.' It takes time and effort and sacrifice. It's messy."[7] I have an additional fear that we are not patient enough with ourselves or with God to allow the necessary time. Are we simply measuring converts or is your church plant prepared to take the time necessary to measure disciples? Are we preparing those born-again believers who have been loved on, mentored, coached and discipled to the point of becoming a serving, following, and reproducing disciple of Christ?

7. Willis and Coe, *Life on Mission*, 99.

Going Hunting or Making Hunters

With fear of alienating some readers at this point I often liken disciple making to hunting. I could take my son or daughter out into the woods at an early age, set them up in the perfect spot, and after listening to enough complaints of boredom, being cold and their great need for snacks I hand them a rifle just in time to shoot a deer or turkey. The thrill and the adrenaline will probably make a convert to hunting. The problem is that there is very little done that day to make a hunter. A hunter will scout locations, consider wind, train their ear, study the times of sunrise and sunset, learn to track animals and develop patience in less than perfect circumstances.

My father, for all his wonderful Christian traits, was a smoker when I was a young boy. When I was twelve and first started to go out hunting, often he would take me out in the woods, sit me next to a tree, stand about twenty-five yards away, and light up one cigarette after another. Needless to say, I never shot a deer as a boy and almost gave up hunting completely because I didn't have anyone to teach me. Several years later I connected with friends who knew how to hunt, pestering them for information, even tagging along whenever possible. I wanted to learn from those who were successful, so I watched training videos, and I read multiple blogs and articles about hunting

I still remember when I personally noticed that I had progressed from a fan in the woods to a hunter. I scouted out some late afternoon travel patterns of deer and selected a nice spot that would afford me a clear line of site and keep me downwind. Squatting behind some small rocks and trees I waited … then I waited some more. Just before sunset, a group of deer moved out from the woods into the clearing I had scouted earlier that fall. They had no idea I was there, and I had all the time in the world to choose the one I felt would feed my family best. I placed my site on the deer of my choosing, slowly pulled the trigger and watched my trophy go straight down.

After some time, I approached my deer to find a clean kill. I was super excited and now needed to figure out how to field dress this animal by myself on the side of a hill. A disheveled looking older hunter walked up on me in the middle of my work. He told me he was on the other side of the hill and heard the shot. Being older I thought he might have some wisdom, so I asked him if he had any recommendations for field dressing. He told me, "No, I've been hunting for over thirty years and never shot a deer." Then he lit a cigarette and watched me finish field dressing mine and prepare it to be taken out of the woods.

Discipleship in our churches is going to involve a strategic plan to develop disciples and even leaders from those who are ready for the work and worthy of imitation. As the Apostle Paul so pointedly proclaimed multiple times in the New Testament, "Imitate me." I think we see a great example for making disciples in his words in Phil 4:17: "Brothers, join in imitating me, and keep your eyes on those who walk according to the example you have in us." Discipleship in the early church had a very apostolic feel to it, as one great example modeled Christ to the next generation of followers. I pray that this is a metric that leads out in your work of church planting. That you do not simply develop one-hit wonders for Jesus but rather you make "hunters", followers of Him with disciple reproduction on their minds. Full seats are nice but are those full seats indicative of the extraordinary mission that we have been given to make disciples?

6

The Extraordinary Body

Maybe you are like me, you were raised in the church and when younger, you never had a full appreciation for the body of Christ. Those folks in your local church were merely excellent bingo players, organ players, or choir leaders. They had their assigned roles in your young mind that consisted of which lady would bring the best snack to Vacation Bible School and which man said the best prayer when the offering was brought forward. You never truly gained an appreciation at an early age for the local church and the amazing people that God used to fill it.

However, I would guess that at some point and time something happened in your life that radically changed your perspective on the body of Christ. Maybe it was still that church you grew up attending or maybe a church you became a part of later in life. The church that moved from being full of quirky people to a church full of incredibly loving and Christlike individuals. A church that wasn't simply a crowd but had become a family, lifting one another up, serving one another and pulling in the same missional direction.

I have been immersed in the church body for a long time. I have witnessed the beautiful workings of this body play out time and time again. I have watched the broken be carried. I have watched the repentant restored. I have watched the isolated welcomed in and the depressed find joy. Like so many other pastors, I have found that the moments when my heart was fullest was when I watched as my church lived out their calling as the body and family of Christ. But in 2016 the family of Christ truly went from being a point of personal pride to a point of personal necessity.

Following the death of my mother several years earlier my father moved from Florida to Pennsylvania to be closer to his children. I was afforded great opportunities to help my dad manage his money, put his life back in order, find him a great apartment in a highly active independent living community and take him to go fish or catch a ball game. He joined our church and immediately began to love on everyone, often using his silly jokes to put smiles on others faces. He asked if he could be used to clean the church on a weekly basis to which I heartily agreed since I knew that serving the church would add a great purpose back into his life. Perhaps the greatest opportunity I had with my father was to invite him into our home in late 2015. The years of having my father close and spending time with him would be cut short after a cancer diagnosis. Dad told me he was scared and unsure of his coming and going sometimes and that living alone made things worse. I watched as my wife and children welcomed him in and as my wife served him and cared for him in some of his darkest moments.

It was late May of 2016 and my wife's cell phone rang in the middle of the night. It was my father calling from his room downstairs. The leukemia that he had been fighting for a year had decided to show its claws. He was calling us to tell us that he needed help getting out of his bed to go to the bathroom. Later we found out that he had bleeding on his spine, leading to the struggle to get up out of bed and go to the bathroom. Having been warned that this kind of bleeding would most likely occur, we were so glad that he was with us and we could help him. It was his last night under our roof.

We were all advised that a rehab facility was needed, so my dad cheerfully obliged much like he did with everything. Our church began to pray for him with more earnestness. I was slated to leave for my first trip to Israel in a few days. Sitting on the edge of my father's bed, I began telling him that I didn't feel right heading off to another part of the world. I told him I was going to cancel my trip. Dad refused to hear it and with a reassuring smile he handed me a check and told me to get nice things in Israel for my family and those in my church family. He loved me and he loved all of them. I hugged him, told him I loved him, told him to get better so he could come home. I told him I'd see him when I got back.

A week later, while sitting on the balcony of my hotel room looking out over Jerusalem, awaiting dinner after a wonderful first day of touring the city, my cell phone rang. I could hear my wife softly crying. "Honey, it's your dad. They found him unresponsive this morning and couldn't wake

him. He had a massive bleed on his brain while he slept. He's gone home."
I cried as my wife firmly convinced me that coming home a few days early
wouldn't change a thing. I looked out over Jerusalem and immediately began to imagine a new city that my father would enjoy and where I could
spend forever with him.

What I soon found out was how important God's family was for me.
My wife was teaching a children's class that Sunday morning when she received the call about my father. She immediately went into a state of panic,
grief and fog. I wasn't there and this added to her state of anxiety. Our
church family swept into action taking over her class, taking her car keys,
driving her to the hospital, taking our children, crying with her and griev-
ing with her. My wife later told me that it was one of the most amazing
times of experiencing church family in her life.

After I returned from my trip, that same church family set in mo-
tion plans and preparations to honor my dad. The necessary logistics for
a memorial service were taken care of and meals were provided. One dear
brother informed me that it is always the pastor who cries with others and
serves them in their time of loss so he felt it was his duty to do that for his
pastor. My entire biological family was floored by their love and compassion. My wife and I each said to the other on more than one occasion, "How
does someone do this without a church body?" Many times after those days
had passed, I was also reminded that this was the loving church body that
God had allowed me to start.

Oftentimes we get focused on so many other priorities and metrics
that we forget the full-scope of a healthy church. We look at full sanctuaries
and declare that church to be healthy. We look at high quality events and
declare that church to be healthy. We look at giving receipts or building
square footage and declare that to be a healthy church. Yet what we forget is
family. Does the body look and act like a family?

Church Planting Metric Seven: Loving One Another

Jesus Christ clearly elevated the importance of interpersonal relationships
among those who would come to follow him. In John 13, Jesus famously
takes up a washbasin and towel and begins to wash his disciples feet. At first
it was confusing to them. They didn't understand the significance of what
he was modeling. Peter famously protested by saying, "You shall never wash
my feet." I can't fault Peter. I think if I was in the same situation, that side of

personal sanctification, I probably would have piped-up as well. As many will attest, I've been known to fire off a quick opinion from time to time without fully thinking things through. I can only imagine what I'd be like apart from the Holy Spirit. Maybe you can relate?

After Jesus is done washing their feet and then explaining his actions, he gives them something new to consider and chew on. Jesus says to those precious ones in that upper room, "A new commandment I give to you, that you love one another: just as I have loved you, you also are to love one another. By this all people will know that you are my disciples, if you have love for one another." (John 13:34–35) In this verse are some very eye-opening realities about this new body we know as the church. The first reality is that loving is a commandment and not a simple choice. Second is that we have a model for doing this in the form of Jesus Christ, himself. Third, the object of our love is one another. In the course of our journey with Jesus, a main outlet for our love is to be the body of Christ. Last is the amazing fact that our witness for Christ increases as a result of our love within the body. In order to hash-out these truths a little more I want to ask some pertinent questions that hopefully will drive you to re-examine this metric in light of your current or future church planting endeavors.

Are you treating loving family as a commandment?

I earnestly believe that a person prioritizes that which is most important to him or her. While I would never say that I have the gift of evangelism, I have always considered evangelism to be the most important thing that a church does. I would even say I went through a period of time when I would place the significance of all the other things that a church does on a level below evangelism. In the deep places of my subconscious, there was a time when I probably would have told you that if forced to choose between crisis marriage counseling and sharing a tract with my waitress, handing over that tract was the better Christian thing to do. This attitude began to filter out into my view of the organized church.

By the time 2006 rolled around and the Lord was sending me off to plant my first church, I was convinced that simply doing more evangelism and discipleship was the only key to opening up the doors of a healthy church. I planted with a team that we convinced to focus every one of their efforts upon successfully sharing the gospel. I think I mentioned earlier that I hate helping people move. I would rather lick 1,000 envelopes an hour at the risk of multiple paper cuts to my tongue than help one person move. Yet that first year of planting I convinced myself that if moving someone might lead to an evangelistic encounter, then strap the piano to my back!

As equally frustrating to me as moving is painting. My wife could walk into the most gorgeous room and quickly surmise reasons that it needed paint. At this point in our life, neither of us has set our eyes on the ceiling of the Sistine Chapel. I am sure that if we did, I would have to talk my wife out of wanting to paint it. In 2007 I allowed someone to talk me into leading our church to paint the exterior of a volunteer firehouse in our community because there was the chance that it would be an evangelistic opportunity. I painted away! The opportunity never manifested itself. The more we pushed our brains to create evangelistic events or programs, the more we spun our wheels. The more we spun our wheels, the more we focused on only evangelistic activities. This cycle went on for a while before some core team members left and I looked around and realized that the fourteen or so we had remaining didn't spend much time together in fellowship. The Lord impressed upon my heart to create strategic opportunities for love and fellowship among the remnant. We created a monthly get-together called Fellowship In Someone's Home (F.I.S.H.) and it was a huge success. We rotated locations, went potluck, and spirits and energy soared!

My problem as a planter and pastor is that I was focused on what I deemed most important and in turn was neglecting those other things that Jesus viewed as important. Loving one another was not optional, it was a command that I learned to gloss over for the sake of trying to create evangelistic opportunities. I don't think it's wrong to paint firehouses, nor do I think it's wrong to hold sports camps to reach children. Just don't ignore what Jesus commands, love for one another where the "one another's" is the body of Christ.

What are we saving them to?

Oddly, the more we loved each other, the more God's people enjoyed being a church. When I preach or teach on the importance of evangelism, I usually spend a few moments stressing the doctrine of repentance. Repentance being that point in which a sinner realizes that they are stuck in sin and no longer desire to walk in sin. They turn in such a way as to exercise faith in claiming the forgiveness of Christ and choose to walk in his ways. While many might nuance their definitions of repentance differently, we can all probably agree that at the point of repentance a person realizes what they are being saved from. Paul put this best by detailing that the wages of sin is death. (Rom 6:23) The result of continuing down the path of sin is eternal death. As the Holy Spirit works on a person's heart during conversion, they realize they want to be saved from death. This is healthy and good.

Once a person repents of their sin, trusts in Christ for salvation and is born-again, they are placed upon a new path, and they are placed into a new family. This family is a large part of what they are being saved to. I often wonder if, for a lack of a better comparison, some new believers show up in our families and immediately begin questioning the adoption agency's decision. Much like my attempt during our firehall painting outreach project, someone encounters Jesus through an evangelistic activity offered by your church plant, only to arrive at a Bible study or church service in which most of the people race out the door when it's over or stand in the corners complaining about the pastor or another member. They punch their attendance card and are never heard from again until the next project or worship service.

I hate to say it, but I believe that the majority of people living in our communities can find a greater level of fellowship from a local bar, a bowling league or even a Moose Lodge than they can at the local church. One of my great fears resulting from the church growth movement is the malaise it has created in those who are being saved into the body. A new believer or someone who is a pre-believer looks at the transient nature and lack of relationship building among those coming and going each week in a church and feels no real connection and no real desire to try and get connected. This stems from lack of avenues for the connection to take place.

The brand-new church in the book of Acts gives us a beautiful description of fellowship. In Acts 2:44–47, a church planter can find hope amidst the ancient text:

> And all who believed were together and had all things in common. And they were selling their possessions and belongings and distributing the proceeds to all, as any had need. And day by day, attending the temple together and breaking bread in their homes, they received their food with glad and generous hearts, praising God and having favor with all the people. And the Lord added to their number day by day those who were being saved.

The hope is found in words like "common", "day by day", and "together". A new church plant is an organism that naturally lends itself to these traits in the early stages. So many pastors quickly become concerned with growth, that they miss out on the joy of solidifying these beautiful traits. The concern over becoming bigger creates an environment where pastors potentially miss the joy of authentic fellowship.

I feel like one of the greatest encouragements that I can give new church planters is to enjoy the loving fellowship. Enjoy the fellowship of forty people. Enjoy the fellowship of two small groups. Enjoy the fellowship of a core-team in your living room. Enjoy the fellowship of celebrating communion while only needing one tray. The more you build your church around the doctrine of true biblical fellowship the stronger your church will become.

Growth in numbers may very well be a result of that fellowship. Since the beginning of God's creation, we have been wired for fellowship. We know from Gen 2:18 that God recognized our need for partnership when he said, "It is not good that the man should be alone." Once people find true community, the very image of God within them craves it. People both inside your church and outside your church are going to find fellowship somewhere. The question is, are they finding authentic biblical fellowship.

I, like many pastors, struggle with the vast array of cultural distractions that steal away our people. With increasing numbers, professing Christians are gravitating towards cycling clubs, youth sports, and season tickets where they tailgate and watch their favorite team each Sunday rather than engaging the church. We have lamented together as we have seen families and individuals go from missing two Sundays a year to missing two Sundays a month within the span of one generation. Our response to this has been to try and outdo culture on its own turf for the sake of growing attendance. We're trying to simply bring people together around the basis of production value, giveaways, or self-help lectures. These cultural tenets may lead to attendance growth but will fall short in the strength of the body.

So how do we define and develop a true community of fellowship? Much has been written on this topic, and I like the way John MacArthur clarifies the true nature of fellowship and gathering in this way:

> There is so much phony fellowship today – people get together on all kinds of pretenses. But the basis of Body fellowship is not the need of the surrounding community, or some common social or religious goal. The basis is found in the word *koinonia*, which

suggests sharing and communion – a common ground. Believers have a common ground, a partnership with something to share.[1]

The way in which your people come to understand the difference between biblical fellowship for which they were created, and that which the world has to offer, is going to begin with your attitude as a planter towards fellowship in the very beginning. You will set the stage for why it is important and how the church prospers as a result of true fellowship.

I am by no means an expert on creating a healthy fellowship dynamic with the church plant body. I can only speak from experience that has involved both successes and many failures. Two simple tactics have risen to the top when it comes to stressing biblical fellowship in your new body. First, I feel that you gain so much long-term goodwill and healthy appreciation for koinonia when you prioritize it from day one. I am a natural introvert so what that means is that one-on-one conversation and chit chat wears me out. I naturally move away from it. But thanks to my business background I have come to understand the value of it. If your core-team is fifteen people, then make a point to invite those fifteen people over… often. Do life together as much as possible. Picnics at the park that include short times of prayer. Christmas parties by the pool (this is obviously a Florida thing) that include a short encouraging devotion. Prayer walking a team-member's neighborhood on a warm summer evening while pushing strollers together. You get the point.

Second, I have found that a new member class has done wonders to solidify biblical fellowship. Some people may be saying to themselves, "New member class? Did this guy crawl out from under a rock? Is he the church's version of Rip Van Winkle?" I get it. Church membership and membership classes have become passe, maybe even going the way of the Dodo. But I do them from the very early stages of church planting because I see them as tremendous opportunities to train and develop churches around the idea of koinonia rather than simply growing anemic churches. Thom Rainer put it bluntly, stating, "I am suggesting that congregations across America are weak because many of us church members have lost the biblical understanding of what it means to be a part of the body of Christ."[2] He later goes on to state that God "placed us in churches to serve, to care for others, to pray for leaders, to learn, to teach, to give, and, in some cases, to die for

1. MacArthur, *The Body Dynamic*, 114.
2. Rainer, *I Am a Church Member*, 5.

the sake of the gospel."[3] Obviously to help others understand these tenets, discipleship is necessary. I have found that a membership class is also a great tool to clarify these expectations. I also utilize membership classes as a way to model fellowship early on. A membership class at my church plant will almost always be in home, it will involve food, it will involve getting to know each other, it will involve praying for each other and it will involve discussing key biblical attributes of a follower of Christ.

Why spend so much time in a church planting book discussing biblical fellowship. Simply put, I believe it is a key missing ingredient among churches today and one of the most important components to your healthy church. A loving body is a body of biblical fellowship. If you have seventy-five people and they are doing life together at a high level then congratulations to you, church planter and pastor. You may have achieved something in an area which a growing number of larger churches are struggling.

Do you operate with a full appreciation of God's economy?

Earlier I mentioned that healthy fellowship may result in growth. I was blessed with a great church planting mentor who had been a church planter himself as well as a pastor and a denominational leader. He had a great knack for taking so much pressure off of me which I had wrongly been placing upon myself. I thought that there was no way that God could save someone for his kingdom unless I was handing out a tract or putting together an outreach program. He kept reminding me of God's economy in light of his sovereignty, often reassuring me that I was functioning under Christ as a church planter, but Christ is both planter and builder. Christ doesn't need me to excel in evangelism in order to draw someone to himself. He is simply asking me to be faithful in all areas. I wasn't being faithful in biblical love and fellowship within the small body that I was given. God can save people if the church is loving each other well; this was my lesson.

A healthy, loving family is evangelism. Remember, in John 13, Jesus told his disciples that they prove to be his disciples by loving one another. Love among the brothers and sisters of Christ puts your friends, family and community on notice that those in your church are living for something greater than themselves. This love communicates the great attribute of sacrifice, and it models a divine agape love that does not come naturally to the world. Love binds together and unifies a people of so many noticeable

3. Rainer, *I Am a Church Member*, 6.

outward differences. To J.C. Ryle the unity amidst difference is the evidence of God and truth of Christianity:

> And yet, notwithstanding all this, there is a marvelous oneness of heart and character among them. Their joys and their sorrows, their love and their hatred, their likes and their dislikes, their tastes and their distastes, their hopes and their fears, are all most curiously alike. Let others think what they please, I see in all this the finger of God. His handiwork is always one and the same.[4]

As you plant a church, build a congregation of love and unity. Trust in God's economy as he draws those in need of salvation even when you are struggling in evangelistic outreach and community engagement.

The words of this book are written in the midst of a worldwide pandemic that is clearly affecting every tiny aspect of our human existence. The pandemic and its effects are so discouraging and nauseating that I had to think twice about whether I even have the stomach to bring it up. I have wrestled with God on more than one dark moment about why he would have me trying to plant a church during this time. Here is how the conversation usually goes down:

Me: "Lord, did you know this pandemic was coming?"

God: "Of course."

Me: "Lord, they didn't teach this in school. I have zero training for this. I'm way out of my comfort zone. I feel like I can't do this."

God: "You can't."

Me: "Lord, I should probably step aside."

God: "And do what?"

Me: (crickets)

Me: "Lord, what do I do?"

God: "Read John 21."

> When they had finished breakfast, Jesus said to Simon Peter, 'Simon, son of John, do you love me more than these?' He said to him, 'Yes, Lord; you know that I love you.' He said to him, 'Feed my lambs.' He said to him a second time, 'Simon, son of John, do you love me?' He said to him, 'Yes, Lord; you know that I love you.' He said to him, 'Tend my sheep.' He said to him the third time, 'Simon, son of John, do you love me?' Peter was grieved because he said to him the third time, 'Do you love me?' and he said to him,

---

4. Ryle, *Practical Religion*, 355.

'Lord, you know everything; you know that I love you.' Jesus said to him, 'Feed my sheep.' (John 21:15–17)

Me: "I'll feed and love your people."

God: "Good."

I have spent way too many days of the pandemic trying to create some sort of church planting miracle. Ultimately, what I keep returning to is loving on God's people, bringing them together around his word and challenging them to remain strong in the faith. I also end up reminding myself of exactly who I am in comparison to who God is. In that, I find great comfort knowing that I serve a God who loves his church more than I ever could. He can move both inside and outside of time and can operate both inside and outside of a pandemic. In turn I have watched my small flock feed hospital employees who were out of work, give needed supplies to teachers returning to a new and strange kind of classroom, supply expecting mothers in crisis with items needed so that they can afford to keep their babies. I have seen a small congregation sit outside through summer heat in Florida so that they might worship together safely, and I have witnessed them continue to pray one for another. I think God is right, I can't but he can.

Now you may be saying to yourself, "I appreciate your encouragement, but you don't know how little I have to work with. I'm at the end of my rope and barely able to put together a core group of people." I do get it. I still find myself in situations where the only way worship happens is if I persuade my daughter to run the media software. Sometimes I have to postpone the start of a bible study because no one wants to come or I don't have the emotional bandwidth to teach a six week class to just one other person. I've watched my kids put away chairs while supposedly committed attenders hurry home to rest. I've shown up expecting a team to help only to stare one other man in the face as I quietly cry out to God, "Now what?"

God's economy says that if you are obedient and faithful in one particular area of life, God can provide fruit and victory in another. God's economy says that the tools required for success on this side of struggle may not be what is needed on the other. God's economy says that praise may be your greatest weapon and that two fish and five loaves can feed the masses. God's economy says that he can unleash the power of his Spirit through a man's hair and that a talking donkey might help put you or someone you love back on track.

One of my favorite examples of God's economy is Joshua and the children of Israel finally crossing into the promised land and beginning to take the land that God promised for themselves. In Joshua 3 we see the faithfulness of God as he leads the Israelites across the Jordan on dry ground. In Joshua 4 the Israelites set up memorial markers to remember the significance of God's work in their lives. In Joshua 5 things get really curious in my eyes. The Israelites reached dry ground and were now camped in the shadow of their enemy's territory. Yet, Joshua leads all the Israelite males in circumcision because he understood the significance of obedience. He would rather have all fighting-age males bloodied and healing, a mere stone's throw away from their enemy than to charge into battle in disobedience. Joshua did this knowing that the fight was the Lord's.

What Joshua didn't know was what had just preceded their act of circumcision. God was already at work. Joshua 5:1 tells us, "As soon as all the kings of the Amorites who were beyond the Jordan to the west, and all the kings of the Canaanites who were by the sea, heard that the LORD had dried up the waters of the Jordan for the people of Israel until they had crossed over, their hearts melted and there was no longer any spirit in them because of the people of Israel." If Joshua was worried about how the victory would occur, he didn't show it. God was already on the move while Joshua was busy practicing obedience. The story ends when God sends the children of Israel out of camp and on a seven-day marching parade around Jericho, ending with trumpets!

Pastor and planter, you have many irons in the fire. You are just one man. You do best to model faithfulness with what you have. Work with what God has given you today. Then trust him and his economy with the results. Your flock is watching you, and they need to believe that God can do a lot with a little. Love them and don't shame them. View them as opportunities for ministry and not merely tools to accomplish something bigger. As the months and years go by tell them the stories of love and obedience from scripture; how God can do a lot through them! I believe he will!

7

The Extraordinary Kingdom

Perhaps it is just me, but it seems like as each generation comes and goes, the viewing of sports changes. Back in the day my father taught me to cheer for every Philadelphia sports team (which really means jeering and booing); he also taught me the great coaches of the day and why they were so special. I can remember sitting in the stands at Veterans Stadium in Philadelphia as a young boy cheering on the "Phightin' Phils" during my first trip to a professional baseball game. I listened as the fans cheered Mike Schmidt when he came to the plate, and a few minutes later as they booed even louder when he struck out. The wins and losses would come and go. Yet when the booing was done, we would walk out of the Vet and I could hear the same fans who just booed the eventual Cy Young Award winner for taking a loss, turn to one another and say, "We got this. We're still a good team." Even in the bad times, the optimism for the team reigned supreme.

Now I watch all different sports with my son (except soccer because it's not a sport). When he was little, I pulled him out of school so we could hitch the train to Penn Station in Philly and ride the subway to Citizens Bank Park to watch the Phils. I taught him to cheer and to boo. We ate soft pretzels on that late Thursday afternoon in May and life was good. I can still hear him yelling, "Go Phillies!" I suppose it worked as they won the World Series that year. His sports viewing has changed through the years. It's not as much about team anymore.

I think he enjoys college football, college basketball and NBA basketball the most. If I were to ask him who is leading the Pacific Division of the NBA Western Conference, he probably couldn't tell me. If I asked him who coaches the reigning NBA champions, he'd struggle to find an answer apart from Siri. However, at eighteen years old he still manages to stay up for the end of games that I no longer can endure. When he wakes the next day, he pulls out his phone to show me some highlight from a crazy Steph Curry three-pointer that occurred on his way to his ninth fifty-point game. To me sports was the team, to my son, sports is Steph Curry. To me, sports was the audacity to throw a slider on a three-two count. To my son, sports is fantasy points.

Please understand, I don't begrudge him this new way of viewing sports because at the end of the day, it is just a game. If he wants to enjoy watching a dunk more than a team victory, so be it. I say, "Enjoy!" However, in this world of instant gratification and television ratings, I miss dynasties and I miss legacies.

Even more, I miss the church which was more concerned about the kingdom than the individual or simply a local church kingdom. I miss the church that was built around a team purpose and not a person's personality. I miss days when success was measured by kingdom metrics and not merely instant numbers.

Allow me to challenge you by saying that Jesus spoke more in his earthly ministry about kingdom than he did about the local church. I am definitely not saying that the local church is not important to Jesus. I have hitched my wagon to starting a local church. However, there must be some significance to Jesus using the word "kingdom" approximately forty-nine times in Matthew's gospel account alone. He blurts out bold kingdom statements such as, "If a kingdom is divided against itself, that kingdom cannot stand." (Matt 3:24) He also said, "Therefore I tell you, the kingdom of God will be taken away from you and given to those producing its fruits." (Matt 21:43) Famously, he also exhorts us by sharing that we are "to seek first the kingdom of God and his righteousness, and all these things will be added to you." (Matt 6:33)

One of the hardest things to do as a church planter is to think with a kingdom mindset. There are multiple reasons for this which I'll share briefly. But first, let me encourage you with the fact that I know what it is like to fight for your very day to day survival. I know what it feels like to watch a family walk out the back door of your new church plant because you don't have the programs they want. Then, like some sort of horrible spiritual hangover, on Monday morning have a denominational leader or partner think they are lifting you up by reminding you to produce more leaders, multiply your small groups and consider making plans early to plant another church. You're just trying to figure out if you're going to have anyone show up to your one existing small group and everyone else is selling you on their church planter leadership development practices.

You want to be that guy. I want to be that guy. I want to read every book with the subtitle called "Mover Shaker Godly Church Planter Guy" and see my picture at the end of each chapter. I want people to come to my church and settle in for a conference on maximizing your everything for Jesus. I want you on stage with me as we present our successes together. But that's not happening right now, you just cleaned the toilet at church and you're now moving on to coaching your one media person to advance the slides before everyone is halfway into the next song verse. You want to develop a media team like the experts say, but everyone else is barely keeping other ministries afloat.

You feel more like a failure than a hero most days. When others talk about kingdom thinking, they refer to how many churches they have started. They share about how many church planters they have mentored and sent out. They astound you with the vast amounts of financial resources being pumped from their church into domestic missions. However, contrary to what you keep telling yourself, you are kingdom-minded. You rolled God's dice and set out to plant a church, after all. Don't sell yourself short and don't expect instant kingdom results that look like everyone else. Trust God in the process and keep one eye on the kingdom goals … while keeping the other on clean toilets.

Economies of Scale

In the world of business there is an economic truth that is readily accepted by all. As a business grows it often becomes more cost efficient for that business to operate. World famous economist, Adam Smith, developed this concept, and it has come to be known as economies of scale. Due to size of production, territorial coverage or a host of other reasons, the cost of doing business decreases as the size of an organization increases. For a small mom and pop business down your street who sells appliances, this means that Best Buy is probably going to always have a cost advantage over them simply because of the warehouse space that affords Best Buy the opportunity to buy appliances from manufacturers in bulk and hold them in ready inventory. Appleton's Appliance Shop doesn't have that same luxury because they can only afford to rent one-twentieth of the floor space as the box store. In tennis terms: "Advantage, Best Buy."

But what does economies of scale have to do with you as a church planter? You don't sell televisions or dishwashers and you're not competing with Amazon or Walmart. I think economies of scale is one of the reasons that church planters don't think with a kingdom mindset. Every example of kingdom thinking that a church planter is asked to consume seems to come from the Walmart's of the evangelical world. The larger the size and numbers, the more effective we perceive a church to be when it comes to the kingdom. Rarely are you going to attend a conference and hear about pastor Barty Shoeffler, who smiled all last year because he witnessed the first small group in his church start a second. Rarely are you going to hear about First Baptist Frackville, and how they doubled their annual financial commitment to overseas missions from $800 to $1600. Nor will you hear about how their new church sent out their first short term mission team of four people.

Yet, Jesus teaches that it's not about the production results, but rather the faith to steward what you do have for the kingdom. In Luke 19:11–27 Jesus shares the parable of the ten minas where the kingdom ruler gives each servant one mina to manage while he is away. It is interesting to note that the only servant chastised is the one who sat on his mina and did nothing with it for the kingdom before the master returned:

> Then another came, saying, "Lord, here is your mina, which I kept laid away in a handkerchief; for I was afraid of you, because you are a severe man. You take what you did not deposit, and reap what you did not sow." He said to him, "I will condemn you with your own words, you wicked servant! You knew that I was a severe man, taking what I did not deposit and reaping what I did not sow? Why then did you not put my money in the bank, and at my coming I might have collected it with interest?" (Luke 19:20–23)

The problem is not in the final numbers, the problem is in the heart of the one who did nothing with what they were given. The goal for each and every church planter should be to keep the stewardship and multiplication of God's resources a priority and not get so caught up in the economies of scale that might reflect in the volume of fruit.

I suspect that another reason that many church planters do not think with a kingdom mindset is concern over personal appearance. It is a lot easier to look the part in today's evangelical culture, especially in the shadow of the church growth movement, when more stuff falls directly under your umbrella. Johnny Hunt refers to leaders as pioneers. No one likes the look of a pioneer when they're in the midst of their challenge. Pioneers move towards a dream and do not concern themselves with appearances. Rarely do they even think of themselves as pioneers, but rather, they are doing what they do out of necessity. They pull a single wagon loaded with their family and their life's possessions across a dusty plain and they smell. Wolves chase them by day and storm clouds by night, and they will never have a comfortable office for which to retreat.

Churches have been glamorizing the comfortable for too long. Don't worry about your appearance but rather, what you are teaching the next generation whom you lead. Hunt exhorts this generation of leader, stating, "You are exploring unclaimed land, wading into uncharted water, and anxious for your followers to see what it looks like out here—out in new vistas where your church, group, or organization has never ventured before. Lead them there. Be a pioneer."[1] Don't allow the perception of kingdom from others to deter you from striking out with your sweaty, dusty, grimy, hard-fought kingdom vision. Rarely do the comfortable change the world, or really change anything at all.

Don't Forget Etsy

When considering your kingdom work it is important to remember this concept of economies of scale because I think it can bring you comfort, and it can also work as a reminder to your purpose. If Walmart and Amazon are hammering mom and pop stores each and every day, then why do those shops exist and why do new ones start in this country with each new sunrise? Honestly, I think it has a lot to do with love and market niche. Opening a thrift store is a labor of love. Owners and operators find themselves working six or seven days a week for years and rarely do they complain because repurposing clothing or household items is a love to them. They know they won't get rich or maybe even achieve the salary of a manager at the local Walmart, yet they labor on because they love it. They also know that no matter what the economy of scale, Walmart cannot sell a single pair of vintage 1980s Jordache jeans, nor can they sell a sweet replica Miami Vice jacket.

---

1. Hunt, *Building Your Leadership Resume*, 194.

It appears that in at least one respect, you as a church planter hold the advantage of Etsy in an everchanging market. My son wanted to buy some things as gifts this past Christmas for those people who are special in his life. He told me that he had already begun to shop around Etsy to find those cool unique gifts that Target and Amazon couldn't offer. This is the beauty of Etsy. Founded in 2005 by Rob Kalin, Chris Maguire, and Haim Schoppik in their Brooklyn apartment, they wanted an online platform that would make it easier for small artisans, craftsmen and entrepreneurs to sell their wares.[2] If you want to buy that special pair of earrings made from the dung of some rare animal, Etsy is your place. If you would like to buy cat toys that are each uniquely embroidered with his or her name, then shop Etsy. Maybe, like me, you're a little more practical and enjoy handmade pens spun from custom wood, then click on Etsy.

I think my son is indicative of this ever-changing culture. It appears that Millennials and Gen Z's are seeking more uniqueness and authenticity in their lives than some of the previous generations. Not only is it refreshing, but it breaks the mold of what had been the predominant kingdom vision of "size" during the Church Growth Movement.

Like we witnessed in Jesus' parable of the minas, any kingdom vision is going to be one of multiplication. Your metrics of relationship building and making disciples are key to this reality as well. With regard to multiplication and the kingdom, Jesus put it this way in Matt 13:31–33:

> He put another parable before them, saying, "The kingdom of heaven is like a grain of mustard seed that a man took and sowed in his field. It is the smallest of all seeds, but when it has grown it is larger than all the garden plants and becomes a tree, so that the birds of the air come and make nests in its branches." He told them another parable. "The kingdom of heaven is like leaven that a woman took and hid in three measures of flour, till it was all leavened."

A mustard tree and a ball of leaven dough both point to the same truth—a little gospel faith now multiplies itself in a fashion that is noticeable. The question for each church planter is, "In addition to multiplying disciples, what does kingdom multiplication look like in my church plant? Is a healthy church merely one that is growing in Sunday worship attendance, or should there be more?"

---

2. Majewski, "A Brief History of Etsy On It's 10th Anniversary", lines 8–11.

Metric 8 – Multiplication of Ministries

The truth about your church plant is that it is more than merely Sunday numbers. You're just often afraid to admit it because other churches don't talk about those things. If it wasn't about more than Sunday numbers you wouldn't be investing your time in recruiting small group leaders, praying about a walk-up food pantry in your lobby or sharing a portion of your offering with the local crisis pregnancy center.

The church plant that I currently pastor is still small in all regards. We're juggling resources from outside partners, congregational giving as well as denominational support. While I'd rather be a fully functioning and self-sustaining church, we're just not there yet. Perhaps you're there now, or you have been. Yet, I have already begun to position my church to multiply itself through advancing ministries in our community. Serving our crisis pregnancy center is one of those key ways in which we advance.

We started in December of our second year, about fifteen months after our public launch, when I asked one woman and one teenage girl from our church to consider kicking off and spearheading our effort to gather some items that would make a difference in the life of a young mother and father who are choosing to keep their baby. We call it our "Thanks for Giving" holiday outreach and it was a success. Each week for one month leading up to Christmas our small congregation brought in supplies such as diapers, wipes, bibs, stuffed animals, onesies, and on and on. That first year we even put ornaments on a small Christmas tree that were labeled with specific ideas for items to bring. The pile under the Christmas tree grew over that month and we were blessed to be able to drop off some amazing stuff in size and scope to the pregnancy center.

By the time we started our next year, we passed our small church budget with an amount designated to help support that same pregnancy center. It isn't much, but our folks love knowing that we put our money and our spiritual feet where our mouth is with regard to protecting the unborn. We now have two members of our church that volunteer at that pregnancy center in an attempt to not only be salt and light but to share Christ with those experiencing crisis in their lives.

The most interesting part of this ministry is where it came from. I speak a lot about God's economy. I mentioned earlier how God can move in one area that is completely opposite to the obedience that we practice in another area. This is his prerogative and I'm so very thankful for it. I was saved as a young teenager, but it was the issue of abortion that challenged me in my area of Lordship. Up until the age of 22 I played a bit of a game with God, fully appreciative of his work on the cross for me but unwilling to commit each and every area of my life to him. I know this could cause some theological debate among some of you, but trust me when I say, I wanted Jesus to be my Lord, but my fingers were still a bit too tight on my own reigns.

This conditional Lordship went on for a bit of time until a friend of mine asked me to go for a run with him. Towards the end of our run, he took his love of politics to a new level with me. He propositioned me with the idea of running for local office. Up until that point we shared similar political leanings, which was one of my reigns. I told him I was intrigued and he began to map out for me a plan that he had clearly already thought through. When he came to the platform of abortion I paused. So big was the pause that it came as a shock to me. He noticed my pause and said, "Is there a problem?" I simply responded with a surrendered heart, telling him that I had never been forced to publicly take a stand on that issue but if forced, I couldn't advocate for choice ... ever. He was offended, broke off the conversation, and I had my first real taste of living out James 2:26, "For as the body apart from the spirit is dead, so also faith apart from works is dead." I had faith, but I needed to work that out now in my own young adult life. I believed that the scriptures taught that life begins at conception (Psalm 139:13) and that each child, whether wanted by their biological parents or not, was created in the image of God. It was at that moment, on that city street corner, that the issue of life caused me to release the grip of all the remaining reigns in my life.

Why does this matter? Because at that moment my openness to God's leading in my life multiplied. At that moment, in God's economy, people I had not even met yet would become disciples of Christ because of my desire to submit to him as Lord in all areas of my own life and ministry. In that moment, people I had not yet pastored would be encouraged to surrender to full-time missions, church planters would be mentored, and my family would hit the domestic mission field. In that moment, the kingdom advanced.

When you plant your church and you see one ministry birthed, and then that ministry births another it may not show up in your annual report. It may not show up in your church budget. It may not even show up in many of your conversations with friends pastoring at larger churches. But from personal experience, trust me when I say, God's kingdom advanced at that moment when a new ministry starts. Is your church multiplying ministries?

From Water Bottles to Living Water

To illustrate the significance of multiplying ministries for kingdom advancement I want to introduce you to Shawna and share her true story. Shawna was a lovely young woman, attending church regularly, and single. She gravitated towards the fairly new singles ministry at our church and probably caught the eye of more than one of the men in their classes and fellowships. The young adults ministry was a new responsibility for me. This blossoming singles ministry as well as the start of a college and career aged group kept me hustling and dreaming. Shawna served here and there and became more faithful. She began to grow in her relationship with Christ and at one point, she realized her need to go public with her faith in Jesus and I had the privilege to baptize her.

When you met Shawna, you would have noticed three things fairly quickly: she was pretty, she was confident, and she was a bit set in her ways. Maybe like me, she still had a good grip on some reigns. She liked her creature comforts and didn't mind admitting it.

A short while after adding a college and career group to our young adult ministry I prayed about whether we should expand the list of ministries to include a foreign mission's trip. My vision was to take some of the young adults from both groups once a year to stretch them for Jesus overseas. I wanted to see them trained in sharing their faith and become more comfortable in evangelism. Our first trip went on the calendar for June to work at a small school in the Dominican Republic. Pause here–––Dominican Republic in June. Shawna was one of the first to sign up. She enjoyed being comfortable and that made me uncomfortable when I saw her name.

Fast forward to the day of departure. Like many short-term mission teams, we rolled up to the departure terminal in a church van. There weren't many of us, but I was optimistic with the twelve that signed up to go. We unloaded and began to get our luggage and passports so that we could line up at the check-in for international departures.

Now I'm not particular about a lot of things. You can give me cheese puffs when I ask for Cheetos. I'll drink a diet Pepsi if my server brings it when I clearly asked for a Diet Coke. I might let you know that you brought me a Pepsi, but I'll drink it. I eat generic marinara and I can shower in the morning or late at night. I don't own a comb (mostly because it's not needed) and I buy most of my fishing gear at Walmart. However, when it comes to traveling by plane, I am particular about being prepared ahead of time. Passport, check! Copies of tickets, check! Stomach medicine, check! I even have a strict personal list of foods that I can and cannot eat within twenty-four hours of takeoff. Shellfish, nope. Eggs, nope. Mexican, nope to the nope. I gave the entire team their restrictions and expectations ahead of time so that there would be no surprises while trying to board an international flight.

Everyone was in good shape. All of the travel documents and passports were accounted for, but we had one bag that was extremely overweight. Shawna was worried that the bottled water that would be available to us in the Dominican would not meet her standards, so she decided to bring her own. She had packed two cases of bottled water into one checked bag. She spent a frantic and excruciating ten minutes trying to decide if she could figure out a way to keep some of her water while meeting the required weight. It didn't happen. The rest of her trip was an eye-opening and, at times, painful experience for her as she came to the realization of true third-world conditions. However, she also fell in love with little children who could care less about her cosmetic regimen or her choice of bottled water. It was a difficult week for her, but I found myself growing in both respect and pride at her ability to adapt. When she signed up the next spring to go to Eastern Europe, I was a little surprised but excited by what God was doing in her life.

Shawna is now an example of the kingdom difference in multiplying ministries, and it happened through God's economy and through no efforts of my own. It always does. An effort to start a short-term mission's emphasis in our church led to a woman who fell in love with short-term missions. Many more trips were in Shawna's future. A young man who had a heart for missions was also in Shawna's future.

You see, God gave me a vision for a new ministry and God gave Shawna and her new husband a heart for the nations. For approximately fifteen years, they have served and raised a family in Africa in an attempt to be the love of Christ while exercising the gifts which God has given them. I have watched them from afar as their precious boys have called a different continent home and those boys have grown to expect to look different from everyone else. They have gone without many creature comforts for years. I suspect that any big budget for cosmetics is long gone. I truly love them for their precious commitment to Jesus. I love that God used a tiny effort on my part to do a kingdom-sized work among the nations to make Jesus famous.

Not a Throw Away

This metric may seem like a bit of a "throw away" metric. It seems like a stretch to say that multiplying ministries within your new church start is in keeping with the evangelistic and missional nature of your call to plant a church. I understand this thinking because I have wrestled with the same thoughts myself. We live in a denominational or partnership-driven world with very real dollars behind those partnerships. Somewhere deep down inside of ourselves we know that sweet old Betty Lloyd is putting a tithe from her social security check in an offering plate somewhere and that money is connected to missions. That money is connected to you. And you feel that her money needs to directly produce salvations, baptisms, and her money needs to put people in the seats.

I encourage you to keep coming back to God's economy. I encourage you to remember that you are a church planter, and not merely an evangelist. We afford many of our foreign missionaries a lifetime to connect with their culture and even start ministries outside the church for the purpose of strengthening the church in their new homeland. We afford them lifetimes to develop livelihoods of the gospel. Sadly, you are planting an American church which often will mean that you don't get that luxury.

Yet as planters we often cling to the story of the early church in Acts 2, and rightfully build our churches around it. It tells us beginning in verse 42 that the new church started eating together, worshipping publicly and privately together, focusing on gathering in each other's homes, and developing ministries of benevolence. Yet, we often forget God's economy in this passage as it closes with Acts 2:47: "having favor with all people. And the Lord added to their number day by day those who were being saved." Let me encourage you with this: you can start a small group ministry among some in your church and God can add salvations. You can worship your heart out each week and God can add salvations. You can start a class to train your first deacons and God can add salvations. Being the church means starting ministries. But also remember that when we act like the church, people notice. Some of those people, God will save.

Church Planting Metric Nine: Multiplication of Leaders

As a child of the eighties, Bill Walsh was the supreme NFL coach. As a boy and later as a teenager I didn't know much about football, but I knew that the Super Bowl meant certain things. First, it meant snacks. Those who know me understand the importance of this statement. Since I was a child, there has been a strange love affair with the potato chip. I'm not here to justify it, nor am I going to try and explain my diet to you. I am simply stating that I grew up in a part of Pennsylvania which has come to be known as "the junk food capital of the world" where potato chips and pretzels are produced at an alarming rate. The bags of chips and pretzels flow through the aisles of supermarkets like chocolate flows through Willy Wonka's factory. I love snacks, buffalo dip, sweet breads, chili on hot dogs, pizza and chicken wings. The Super Bowl is God's kindness to me when it comes to those things that I enjoy so much!

Second, the Super Bowl meant friends. I can still envision myself as a fifteen-year-old boy with my legs hanging over the arm of a recliner. I can still hear the banter back and forth with my friends about the game as we threw popcorn or pizza rolls at each other. I can feel the sting of the cold air and often, the snow, as we would head outside at halftime to throw the football up and down the street. As a nineteen-year-old I can remember the agony on that special Sunday night of having to leave home and leave my friends (like that girl that had my eye) in order to make the two-hour drive back to the Penn State campus and resume my studies. The Super Bowl always brought out the joy of unfiltered friendships and time spent simply enjoying each other. It is still special to me because of this.

Third, the Super Bowl usually meant Bill Walsh. As coach of the San Francisco 49er's, Walsh appeared in three Super Bowl's between 1982 and 1989. He won all three. Other coaches like Dan Reeves, Don Shula and Joe Gibbs made multiple appearances as well, but it was Walsh who dominated the landscape because his teams always won. Seriously, who will ever forget the images of Joe Montana and Bill Walsh talking strategy on the sideline?

However, what makes Walsh truly special actually isn't his Super Bowl appearances and wins. Other coaches, like Chuck Noll, have more. It isn't his total number of wins, either. Don Shula has more. It isn't even his innovative west coast offense. It has been both praised and lampooned through the years. Most experts inside and outside of football would tell you that what makes Bill Walsh truly great is his legacy of coaches.

From one man has come two generations of coaching leaders that reads like a who's-who of playoff and Super Bowl greatness. Names like Holmgren, Green, Reid, Billick, Shanahan, Mariucci, Gruden, Fisher, McCarthy, and Harbaugh just to name a few. I'm not a walking football dictionary but even I know that the legacy of names is impressive. Walsh appeared in and won those three Super Bowls, however 43 percent of the other fifty-one Super Bowls have been won by Walsh or someone from his coaching tree.[3] I don't care what industry you are in, that kind of legacy is mighty impressive!

As a church planter, most days you will feel less like Bill Walsh in the Super Bowl and more like Pee Wee Herman trying to run a Pop Warner league summer tryout. You'll be thinking less about legacy and more about trying to find a pair of shoulder pads to fit a six-year-old wide receiver. You have twenty people on your core team and your life is consumed with casting the vision or teaching the playbook. Creating a legacy of leaders through multiplication is almost impossible to get your mind around. I'm with you. So haunting is the reality of this to me, I spent a great deal of time in a doctoral program trying to figure out better ways for church planters to develop leaders. At times I would feel encouraged in my progress and at other times I felt like I was trying to drive up an icy driveway in a rear-wheel drive automobile.

Yet, when you are tempted to keep telling yourself that you'll work on leadership development later, perhaps after you become an established church, I want you to consider the words of John Maxwell: "Too often leaders put their energy into organizations, buildings, systems or other lifeless objects. But only people live on after we are gone. Everything else is just temporary."[4] The findings of missiologist and former church planter, Ed Stetzer, also flesh out the practical importance of church planters and their need to develop leaders. He notes that in a study on church-plant survivability, 68 percent of church plants still survive at year four.[5] The same study reveals the "odds of survivability increase by over 250 percent where leadership development training is offered within the plant."[6] Maxwell's

---

3. Whiteford, "The 'Bill Walsh Model' to Your Leadership Legacy", line 39.

4. Maxwell, *The 21 Irrefutable Laws of Leadership*, 260.

5. Stetzer and Bird, "The State of Church Planting in the United States: Research Overview and Qualitative Study of Primary Church Planting Entities", 2.

6. Stetzer and Bird, "The State of Church Planting in the United States: Research Overview and Qualitative Study of Primary Church Planting Entities", 7.

words and Stetzer's results should challenge each church planter to think about a process for training leaders before beginning the actual process of planting a church.

Now, let's just get this out there—out of all the things I can do as a church planter, this is the hardest and requires the most effort on my part. I naturally gravitate towards starting small groups and teaching. I love planning for a worship service launch. I get kicks out of planning a series of sermons for that launch. I even enjoy scouring local real estate looking for places to meet. Multiplying leadership out of yourself and your newest fellow leaders is unnatural to most church planters and a little unnatural to the environment to which many of us find ourselves on a daily basis. As mentioned before, I find great pleasure in mentoring and developing leaders, it is just going to feel difficult if not impossible in the early stages of church planting. Your heart is going to want to develop leaders, but the urgency of your to-do list is going to demand that you find a halfway decent worship leader that doesn't spout or sing heresy.

Yet, I think that Jesus can work even in the urgent. It may just require some creativity, flexibility and devotion on your part—especially early on. When you consider the ministry and work of Jesus, your mind may not immediately gravitate towards his leadership development. Yet, leadership expert, Ken Blanchard refers to Jesus as the greatest leadership role model of all time.[7] His development of leaders seems to predate his outward signs and miracles, his sanctifying work of the cross, and his launching of the church. I'm not saying that this order dictates levels of importance, I'm merely pointing out the value that Jesus recognized in developing a group of twelve men to become the leaders that the future church would need.

It is difficult to get to that place of leadership development. We all love the idea of a ministry that is run by someone else who is actively training another person to take their place or start more ministries. This is the heart of discipleship as well as leadership. I would submit that every disciple-maker is a leader. Looking again at Jesus' words to the woman at the well, we know that his kingdom goal is multiplication in our lives, a drink that leads to a wellspring in each of us. (John 4:14) That which is "kingdom" in us will become "kingdom" in others.

That being said, you've probably have many irons in the fire and you're too tired or busy to do leadership development at a high level. Let me set you free—I'm not necessarily asking you to do it at a high level, I'm just

7. Blanchard, *Lead Like Jesus*, 9.

proffering the idea that you start. I have to convince myself each and every day to take what I've been given and start somewhere, as well. Sadly, in many ways the evangelical church in America has spent the past several generations putting every activity that we do into a program, kit or class. I don't think your leadership development needs to be this way. Actually, I think you might find it to be healthier and more relational if you don't do it this way. Rather, take a little effort to stir the water and watch what God can begin to do in a few of your folks. Even though my intent is not to write a "how to" book, I humbly submit three rather organic steps you can try.

First, pray for leaders and then invite others to join you in that prayer. Consider Jesus' initial step before choosing the twelve. Luke 6:12–16 illuminates his prayer process:

> In these days he went out to the mountain to pray, and all night he continued in prayer to God. And when day came, he called his disciples and chose from them twelve, whom he named apostles: Simon, whom he named Peter, and Andrew his brother, and James and John, and Philip, and Bartholomew, and Matthew, and Thomas, and James the son of Alphaeus, and Simon who was called the Zealot, and Judas the son of James, and Judas Iscariot, who became a traitor.

Jesus took the time to get alone with God and petition him. He took serious time and effort in prayer before choosing the twelve to be appointed as the future leaders of the church. I would encourage you to do the same. My prayer journal is full of names for various reasons, and potential leaders is one of those reasons. It may be birthed out of a perceived need, a growing relationship or even a struggle that I was having. Inevitably as I pray for leaders, God gives me names and God gives me potential purposes. I know it doesn't seem like the kind of thing that will launch your next great conference break-out session, but first stir that water by petitioning God on behalf of those whom he could use as leaders. I would also suggest that you include your church or core team in on this prayer. Let them know that it is your vision to raise up, develop and multiply leaders. Ask them to begin joining you for those who could be a part of such an adventure. You might be surprised how quickly, when praying, even a small group can catch on to the vision and begin to see themselves in that role. I've always found it difficult to pray for laborers in the harvest and not at least consider myself for that role of laborer. (Luke 10:2)

Second, invite those people to join you on the leadership development journey. You don't know until you ask. Asking is stirring the water and that is moving the kingdom forward a little at a time. You may get some "no" answers and that's fine. You want those who are committed. My pastor friend, Ed, used the phrase "pushing a rope" quite often. It was his way of referring to the efforts of pastors to try and get uncommitted people to do something. For example, you and I are committed to getting the dishes in your dishwasher as clean as possible hence we take care in how we load it. Our teenagers have zero commitment to ensuring clean dishes. This shows in the effort they put forth in loading the dishwasher. I always stand amazed when I look at the results after asking them to do this simple task. No matter how many times I explain it, if they don't care, it will show in the results. All that said, you don't need warm bodies for your next generation of leaders, you need committed souls.

Third, model and mentor with purpose. Maxwell went on to discuss how existing leaders go on to grow in their legacy and how leadership development becomes a part of that. His progression for leaders is the following four steps:

- Achievement comes when they do big things themselves.
- Success comes when they empower followers to do big things for them.
- Significance comes when they develop leaders to do great things with them.
- Legacy comes when they put leaders in position to do great things without them.[8]

You can see the progression from doing big things themselves to developing the kind of leaders who do great things without them. So much about our social media culture continues to put us at the center of everything, but a biblical legacy is one that takes people and develops them in a way that another person's success without your recognition is actually your greatest success.

Herein lies the beauty of Jesus' day to day, earthly ministry. It was modeling and mentoring with a purpose. I love the image of Jesus roaming around the Galilean countryside and small towns with his rag-tag group of disciples. In that group were these twelve men who were not only being

8. Maxwell, *The 21 Irrefutable Laws of Leadership*, 260.

taught by him, but were also doing life together with him. They watched him heal the sick, he taught them how to pray, and he modeled forgiveness and unconditional love. He then sent them out. In Luke 10 we even read of Jesus sending out seventy-two others ahead of him in groups of two to do that which he had been modeling. They come back joyously testifying to the great things that occurred through their ministry, yet Jesus cautions them against their own pride. (Luke 10:17–20). Jesus even makes the effort to take along his inner three (Peter, James and John) to join him on that mountain as he was transformed before their eyes and converses with Moses and Elijah. Jesus did this knowing that Peter would speak out of turn. Yet it left such an impression on Peter that it continued to impact him well into his ministry:

> For we did not follow cleverly devised myths when we made known to you the power and coming of our Lord Jesus Christ, but we were eyewitnesses of his majesty. For when he received honor and glory from God the Father, and the voice was borne to him by the Majestic Glory, 'This is my beloved Son, with whom I am well pleased,' we ourselves heard this very voice borne from heaven, for we were with him on the holy mountain. (2 Peter 1:16–18)

The leadership of the church is one of Jesus' great legacies as he took tedious care to pour himself into others all the while knowing that his mission was more than that.

You can see the great legacy of leadership development in Paul's life as well. His pastoral epistles spell this out, especially to Timothy and Titus. Timothy traveled back and forth with Paul, witnessing the abuse, the heroics, the movement of God's hand in Paul's life and the commitment to the gospel. When it came time to develop leadership in the churches at Ephesus, there was such great trust and love towards Timothy that Paul felt confident in allowing him to do the work of developing leaders. The mentor wasn't even there, he simply surrendered his written words of encouragement and instruction. He tells his child in the faith in 1 Tim 4:11–12, "Command and teach these things. Let no one despise you for your youth, but set the believers an example in speech, in conduct, in love, in faith, in purity." He reminds him to fight the good fight of faith (1 Tim 6:12) and to guard the good deposit entrusted to him (1 Tim 6:20). These are words of a man who is fully invested in the life and ministry of someone he has mentored and cared for over the years.

I pray that rather than simply developing a program in your church plant you develop relationships. That they would be relationships that last a lifetime and that you have opportunity to pour yourself into others who in turn do the same. I have been the beneficiary of two men who have done exactly that. I wasn't viewed as a notch in their gun belt or simply a tool to accomplish some ministry purpose. When I was first called into ministry, one man took me everywhere and showed me everything, even as an unknown entity. He allowed me to try, fail, and try again. He championed my successes and softened many of the blows from my failures and he always communicated unconditional love to me as a next-generation leader. Another man met me where I was as a potential new church planter and made me feel significant. He challenged my thinking and pushed me in my abilities. He showed me the way, prayed with me in my heartaches, and continued to assure me along the way. If there were ever two men who I would call legacy builders, it would be these men.

May you be such a legacy builder, and not simply a church planter or team member or pastor. As Maxwell said, people live on after we are gone. Invest in people, multiply leaders. I'm a believer that by making this investment, you will find some of the greatest fulfillment of your life.

Church Planting Metric Ten: Multiplication of Churches

Allow me to share with you part of Kurt's story. Kurt was a church planter who arrived in a new town and was brimming with optimism. He had spent months praying about his new community and praying for ways in which he could start a new church that would be intentional about reaching the lost and making disciples for Jesus. On top of that, Kurt had a vision for being a church that would be part of a movement to see dozens of new churches planted across his region. Crazy right? Kurt actually thought he could be an initiator as part of a church planting movement.

When Kurt arrived in his new hometown, he got his family all settled in and as one of his first priorities he decided to try and set up a meeting with the only other pastor from his denomination. He first emailed the medium-sized First Baptist Church and attempted to set up an appointment with their senior pastor to introduce himself, share a little bit about what he was doing and to pray for both of their ministries. The email went without response. A second email went without response.

Kurt, not yet jaded with any kind of church planting cynicism, thought that maybe he had a bad email address or that the email landed in a junk folder. He decided to go neanderthal and pick up the phone to make a call. When he did, a receptionist answered and upon Kurt's explanation, she acted as confused as Lawrence Welk at a Metallica concert. He would have had more success explaining cheese on the moon instead of church planting. The receptionist offered to pass a message along to the senior pastor's assistant who would return the call. The call never came.

Kurt didn't feel right planting in town with an existing Baptist church without at least a conversation, so he tried one last time to reach the senior pastor. He managed to find his direct email address. Kurt invited him for coffee and conversation. After a few weeks the pastor wrote back and told Kurt he had a few minutes available next Tuesday in his office. It wasn't the vibe Kurt was going for, but he would take what he could get.

The day of the meeting came, and after parking his car he wandered into the reception area and was eventually ushered into the senior pastor's office. They shook hands, before Kurt was offered a seat and a chilly, formal conversation ensued. Kurt felt like a fish out of water. It was clear that the pastor of First Baptist was not interested in a new church in town even though the growth of the community told him that if every existing church doubled their sanctuary size, there still wasn't enough room for all the lost residents. He was worried that maybe he wasn't as welcome as he thought and starting a church planting movement was a vision in his head alone.

As the meeting came to a close, he could tell the senior pastor at First Baptist wanted to be anywhere else but there and before he could offer to pray for that pastor and their church he was shown the door. On the way out, he asked the pastor if he had any advice about pastoring in this new community. His parting word to Kurt summed up the meeting well. He said, "Yes, don't try and start a church by the interstate, we're going to build a campus there." Kurt's heart sank, and his cynicism for kingdom growth reared its ugly head for the first time in this new venture.

Sadly, planting a church in the shadow of the church growth movement is going to present all of us with some painful obstacles. Planting a church that plants churches may, initially, make you feel like Lawrence Welk at a Katie Perry concert. You'll have defeatist thoughts like, "Why think multiplication when this community doesn't even want one church?" You'll find yourself using church growth metrics to justify why you're not able to engage early on in starting more churches. You'll find yourself adopting the mentality of that FBC pastor without putting out any effort to do the impossible.

There are very few opinions in my head regarding an ideal size for a local church. Like most pastors, I am always full of opinions and like most pastors, I can find scripture to support my opinion. When it comes to congregational size, I'm at a loss to defend the preferred girth of a church one way or the other. When people ask me how big I want our church to become, I usually give the pithy, yet honest answer, "That's up to God." One of my significant struggles with a purely church growth movement in America is that bigger churches is all that we have gotten and new, planted churches were lacking. Sure there were some, back when greater than 50 percent of church plants failed.

The need for new churches, even in one single community, is great. As Paul took the gospel to Asia and Macedonia and elsewhere the gospel he shared took root in the form of churches. The epistle that we read today is a letter that he wrote to "churches" in Galatia. (Gal 1:2) One region, multiple churches. In this practical, and what we see as "highly evolved" world, what benefit is it to continue to strive for an explosion of unique ekklesia communities of faith? Common sense should tell us that as communities grow, lostness increases, and preferences change. The danger in this for a single church is that they start to perceive their turf and their singular vision as God's turf and God's only vision.

I tend to think that multiplying ourselves through the starting of new churches is opening ourselves up to God's unique and sovereign purpose on his turf. One church does not hold ownership over his turf. Jeff Christopherson offers this challenge, stating:

> What if we drew the lens back all the way until we came face to face with the obvious truth that the Sovereign God, the King of His Kingdom, is not dependent on or limited in any way by me or my tribe? He alone holds claim to the turf of His Kingdom. He is not looking for sides to join. He is seeking a people who will lay aside every other allegiance (including religious ones) and unite with Him.[9]

With each new autonomous church comes the potential to reach a people group, a community, a niche that no longer jives with our programs, tactics or methods. Shocking as it may sound, pastor, your preaching may not reach everyone. And that's not because you lack enough podcasts and

9. Christopherson, *Kingdom Matrix,* 75.

livestreams. They simply may not like you or your style. Gasp! And that singing Christmas Tree your choir has done every year since 1957, might not connect with about 85 percent of your neighborhood population. Shocking, I know.

You Can Do A Lot With A Little

So how do I go about engaging in church multiplication when I am fighting for the very life of my little church plant right now? I like this question because I believe, like so many God-sized things, the answer is made up of one small part practical and one large part faith. From my humble experience, there are certain things that can be done during different stages of your church plant that continue to stir the waters, trust in God's economy and position your people for a movement of God.

First, church plant multiplication must be part of what you communicate from the beginning of your own church start. And by beginning I mean, like when you are sipping those cups of coffee at your first exploratory meeting or first community bible study or host group. Sew into your story the need for many more churches across your county, state and globe. Plant into the brains of your team of initiators the idea that we are a sent people living for a sent purpose. Teach them the book of Acts early on and in those teachings, point out new church starts, churches helping churches, and the power of personal evangelism. I have always tried to do a vision message at the beginning of each new year. I speak to the big picture of our overall ministry, challenge our people in our progress, emphasize sharing the gospel one-on-one (again), and I always include the role our church has to play in starting new churches.

Second, budget for kingdom investments. It will be a lot easier to help fund your own church plant or maybe help pay another church planter's salary down the road if you are financially committed to doing something early on. It doesn't have to be an overly complicated commitment, but your folks should notice that domestic missions and church planting is a priority in your small or modest budget. For our churches, we have always started by setting aside a certain percentage of our offerings to go directly to the agencies that fund both foreign missions and North American church planting. We have historically put in small amounts to send to approved new churches starting in our area. It may only be $75 or $150 a month but your people will begin to see it as part of their kingdom identity.

Third, don't devalue mentoring and let your church know that you do it. You may not be able to put a big financial dent into the budget need of the new church plant or multiple plants you wish to help but you have more than money to offer. You have experience, wins and losses, practical resources and most importantly, a listening ear. In keeping with the importance of multiplying leaders, you can offer mentorship and your personal time to a new church planter trying to navigate his own landscape. Your encouragement and advice can be just as valuable in the beginning as the financial resources that he receives. Maybe your denomination has a role you can play by helping to train future planters? Just begin to stir the water and see what happens. Some of my most treasured times have been with men who were called to plant a church and God allowed me to be a voice in their lives. To this day, a few of them are still some of the closest friends I have. Most importantly to this third point, share with your congregation the names of the planters you're working with and share the appropriate stories of the times that you spent with them.

Fourth, include them as part of your regular personal and congregational prayer. I love praying for new planters by name. I love getting to know their spouses and children and praying for them as well. For years the churches I have been a part of have maintained a weekly email prayer list. The list includes praises, congregational prayer concerns, prayers for lost friends, neighbors and loved ones as well as the names of church planters, their families and their churches. The planters who I mentor, train, and eventually those our church supports are names that are familiar to everyone because they have been praying.

Fifth, when the time comes, become a sending church. Keep one eye on your leaders for potential planters. Keep the other eye out for potential planters within your outside circles of influence like sister churches, the youth director down the street or even an old buddy from seminary. When the time is right, be prepared to unleash your church as an all-encompassing training center for church planters and a safe-haven for their families. I'm so thankful for the financial resourcing that comes from my existing sending church, but I equally love the safe-haven it has become. It has provided a youth ministry for my teenagers before we had one. It has provided men and women who speak into my children's lives. It has provided a place to vent. It has provided a plethora of prayer supporters. It has provided office space away from my home. It has provided ideas and fellowship. Being a sending church is really about being a training ground and lifeline for the next generation of planters. When it's time, don't be afraid to step up to the plate financially and seek kingdom-sized commitments for at least four to six years from your folks to make that new church go.

The kingdom of God demands churches that think in a kingdom way. You are not planting your kingdom, rather, you are involved in one part of a kingdom-sized work led by a God who is thinking above and beyond what you could possibly be imagining for yourself right now. I have found that the more you keep your allegiance to the kingdom, the easier it is to navigate disappointment and doubt and the more fruitful you will feel. Kingdom thinking is also a reminder that my ministry doesn't have to look like everyone else's, it simply needs to look like God's fingerprint.

8

Moving Forward

Three Yards and a Pile of Dust

BY THIS POINT IT should not come as a surprise to you that I am a huge fan of football. Actually, one of my great regrets in life is that I never played organized football. I've always been a fairly tall guy so before I had much knowledge or interest in football my dad took me out to experience a youth football practice when I was in eighth grade. I remember the smell of the old used equipment as they sized me up and put on the pads. It was a strange mix of body odor and some sort of stale mildew smell. My father had a friend who was the youth coach and when I walked on the field he sized me up and said, "Linebacker for sure!" The sad part was, at age twelve, I had no clue what a linebacker did other than play defense.

After a couple hours of up-downs, being yelled out and trying to figure out different positions I decided that maybe football wasn't for me. Now I look back and wish I had waited it out a bit longer and truly found a position I love because the strategy and passion of football is first rate, with baseball being a close second.

Fast forward and I choose to attend college in the Big Ten. If you know anything about football, the Big Ten should conjure up images of Woody Hayes, The Big House in Michigan, sub-freezing kickoffs, Paul Bunyan's Axe, and white helmets and black shoes. It should also conjure up an image of a style of football that is pound and grind on the ground. For years, Big Ten fans have known this to be a style of football that is "three yards and a pile of dust". When I married a girl from the Southeastern Conference she cringed at this style of play, however, in places like "The Shoe", "Happy Valley", and Camp Randall it is cherished, appreciated and expected.

There is nothing like watching a team assert themselves on the ground throughout the course of a football game as they rattle off two, three, four yards each carry. This style of play wears down the opponent both mentally and physically. It is an assertion of power and will and begins to cause the opponent to think less of themselves. The ground game is about consuming the entire clock, controlling the football and winning. Period. A team that has been run over for four quarters and loses by six points can often feel more humiliated and exhausted than a team that lost by twenty-five to a "quick-strike" offense. I have come to fully appreciate three yards and a pile of dust. This type of success doesn't happen without a total team effort.

While moving forward in church planting or ministry in general, you are going to feel an incredible amount of pressure to throw the ball deep each and every day. You are going to feel pressure to make questionable stewardship decisions for the sake of meeting someone's timetable or perhaps simply a countdown clock in your own head. Moving the kingdom forward is not set to a clock. Your church plant is going to be successful because of two factors: Christ's work and your faithfulness. Do not be afraid of three yards, do not be afraid to win the game by a field goal, and do not be afraid of the hard road or running between the tackles.

Prestige or Persistence

Church planting has been my life for a while now. I've become accustomed to the fact that there will probably be little prestige in my future. I'm not going to speak at a large conference. I'm not going to be called upon to put together a "how-to" kit or program. I don't know many famous people. I met Dr. J once but that doesn't really count because he won't remember me and this conversation is about church planting which he doesn't do. Perhaps better than that, Billy Graham did wave at me and even said "hello" as well, but I'm sure he didn't go home and immediately tell Ruth about it. I earned a doctorate, but all that means is that I'm broke more than I'm prestigious. If you're looking for prestige and you're considering church planting or just starting your plant, you might want to reconsider.

I have found that church planting (for most of the planters that I have met) is about persistence rather than prestige. Persistence is about using all four quarters in order to assert the will of the coach according to the giftings of your team. Persistence doesn't quit if the drive is halted at the fifty-yard line. Persistence is a lot of pep talks, team motivation, and dirt. So dirty has been much of my church planting experience that I have become unreasonably cynical of shiny things in the church. I often joke about how my entire budget is much less than what the church down the street spends on new lighting each year. I'm not saying it's right, but it might be how a fullback views the star wide receiver.

Persistence is often about a little more pain as well. Watching a running back or fullback get stronger as the game rolls on is only telling half the story. Each Sunday or Monday morning those players try to put their feet on the floor and hobble to the breakfast table because of the amount of shots that they inflicted on others in order to be persistent in their game plan. Persistence will mean practicing all week with bruises from last week. Persistence means accepting that which is painful and using it as motivation.

I marvel at so many of the great saints that have come before me in the work of missions and church planting. As you move forward, I just can't emphasize enough the benefit that you will find to your work by reading and studying some of the great names of missions work as well as other heroes of the Christian faith. People like Jim Eliott, Adoniram Judson, David Brainerd and William Carey will help put perspective to the day-to-day work that you do.

Accepting Pain as Part of Your Process

We don't like to talk about pain. It is not in keeping with the western church to view pain as part of God's process. It's certainly not part of the prosperity gospel theology that many have accepted in the western church. Yet pain is a fairly consistent thread among the lives of those who have done so much for the kingdom. I should say, pain and persistence.

Take David Brainerd for example. Born in Connecticut in 1718, he was frail, sickly, and expelled from Yale for being too critical. He died at the age of 29 from tuberculosis.

Even though he was rejected by his contemporary mission sending agencies, he became a missionary to the American Indians across the Northeast. He was persistent despite his pain and disappointment.

The miraculous working of God in Brainerd inspired the great revivalist preacher, Jonathan Edwards, who eventually wrote Brainerd's biography.

That same biography of persistence amidst pain and struggle ended up in the hands of bunches of aspiring Christians such as William Carey. Carey read Brainerd's biography and he was changed. He bought in to persistence rather than prestige.

Carey is often thought of as the father of the modern missionary movement, yet his road was anything but prestigious. In his 1836 memoir on William Carey, Francis Wayland said, "Like most of the master minds of all ages, Carey was educated in the school of adversity."[1] Dr. Danny Akin says,

> There were times when his soul was plunged to the depths of depression. He would bury two wives, with his first, Dorothy, sorrowfully, going insane. He would bury three children, and certain others disappointed him. He lost most of his hair due to illness in his early twenties, served in India for forty-one years never taking a furlough, fought back dysentery and malaria, and did not baptize his first Indian convert, Kirsha Pal, until his seventh year in the field![2]

When I consider persistence with regard to the work of the gospel it is the names of Brainerd and Carey that come to my mind. However rewarding persistence may sound on some level, pain rarely sounds the same.

Personally, I tend to run from pain. I am known to get "man fevers" according to my wife, which is basically the same as a dripping nose and a constant barrage of overreactions like, "Honey! Feel my forehead. I'm not doing well at all. I need to lie down." To be honest, a hangnail can put me down for a good long time. I can stare at a papercut long enough I've convinced myself that a stitch or two might be necessary. But joking aside, pain in the ministry of missions and church planting is going to be your calling. Persistence in that pain is going to be your witness.

In your pain and struggle will arise character and an identity that will speak louder than you ever could on your own. One scriptural account that has always been a real challenge to me is found in Acts 5. The high priest has the Apostles arrested for preaching Jesus. An angel frees them and commands them to go preach some more. The Apostles are rounded up once again. Then, after much debate, the high priest orders them to be beaten and released. Here in lies the hard teaching:

---

1. Sutton, *A Matter of Conviction*, 59.
2. Akin, *10 Who Changed the World*, 9.

and when they had called in the apostles, they beat them and charged them not to speak in the name of Jesus, and let them go. Then they left the presence of the council, rejoicing that they were counted worthy to suffer dishonor for the name. And every day, in the temple and from house to house, they did not cease teaching and preaching that the Christ is Jesus. (Acts 5:18—21)

I am not saying that you and I are the modern day equivalent of Peter or John. We are not Apostles, but we do carry the apostolic message of freedom in Christ alone. Do we count ourselves worthy to suffer? Or, rather, are we public martyrs or perhaps we make our ministry about our difficulties rather than the power of God that goes well beyond our pain?

Your pain may look like a belligerent or accusatory church member. Your pain may consist of lies or accusations that are made as an attempt to attack your character. Your pain may be actual, physical pain. I know that my body is quite different in the midst of my second church plant than it was fifteen years earlier when I started my first. To stand and greet visitors from the community at an outreach event that lasts hours is going to eventually mean multiple nights of back pain and little sleep. I have had to prepare myself for it. I don't claim to know your pains but I do know that in the pain process comes the very visible manifestation of the grace of Christ. It might be one of your greatest witnesses as a church planter.

No Time on Deserted Islands

You probably have a list of movies that you can watch over and over again. You may get made fun of for it, but you just don't care. If you're a man, your list might include Steel Magnolias, Sophie's Choice or The Notebook. I'm thinking, however, that your list is probably more like mine: The Patriot, Gladiator, and Dumb and Dumber. On my list, I also throw in Cast Away. Perhaps it is some sick fascination with the crash of that doomed FedEx plane. Over the years, however, I have actually come to appreciate it on an artistic level. I love that Tom Hanks does the majority of the film alone. I find it fascinating that Hanks' character, Chuck, chose to keep several packages for delivery as a symbol of his hope in returning home.

Perhaps the biggest artistic point that jumped out to me was Hanks' choice whether to leave the island not just in body but later in spirit. After his rescue, many funny scenes ensue such as a huge party thrown by FedEx in his honor where he looks over a massive amount of party food spread out over a large table knowing that just days ago he was struggling to find a single thing to eat. He knew that all the food was going to be thrown away. After the crowd leaves, he grabs a crab leg, and with a bit of disdain after years of eating crab, tosses it aside.

It is after the party when Chuck finds himself alone once again in a hotel room. Rather than sleeping on the bed he chooses to curl up on the hard floor to try and find sleep. Sleep doesn't come. He has spent so long on the island, uncomfortable by himself, all he knows is to revert to his nature. However, the movie ends with Chuck sniffing the aroma of life amongst humanity once again. The last scene shows our protagonist sitting in his Jeep at a fork in the road. We get the impression that he chooses people, relationships and life.

Now, you may find my artistic interpretation of Cast Away as a bit much, but I think it illustrates a larger point with regard to your life as a church planter. It is an experience that can easily leave you on a deserted island. Not only are you beginning a kingdom work with very little built-in church family, but you are most likely doing it in a new community where you have yet to meet many people. You are also doing it with a level of stresses that few will be able to relate to and stresses that often tie directly to the people you are trying to minister to. Your island can lead to increased depression, loneliness, isolation and even strain on your marriage and within your family. It can cause you to place a burden upon the relationship with your wife that she is not, perhaps, ready to carry. I remember during the early years of each church plant looking back longingly for the fellowship that I once had with other pastors and staff members at a previous church. However, I knew that those days of staff interaction may be a while in coming if they would come at all. So, I had to choose whether to continue to sleep alone on the floor or move on in my spirit to get off my island.

Over the years I have found a couple of key difference-makers when it comes to paddling off your island. First, it is important to develop a network of pastors and church planters that you meet with regularly. Your super-spiritual side will push back against this because you will envision some sort of accountability group or formalized discipleship group. That's not what I'm getting at here. I'm talking about a group of guys that understand your ministry and the affect it has on our lives. These are guys who are experiencing some of the same things and don't expect you to be John Wayne.

I've learned that when I try and navigate church planting alone, it creates a downward spiral in my life that is hard to reverse. Paul Tripp said this about his own ministry life and the important lesson he learned about having a community:

> I have now come to understand that I need others in my life. I now know that I need to commit myself to living in intentionally intrusive, Christ-centered, grace-driven, redemptive community. I now know it's my job to seek this community out, to invite people to interrupt my private conversation, and to say things to me that I couldn't or wouldn't say to myself.[3]

I've learned, like Tripp, that I (like all church planters) must create community especially when your church community is small or non-existent. I have worked, sometimes harder than I should have to, to connect with other guys in my community who have also put their hand to the plow. At least once a month I meet face to face with fellow planters or pastors for a lunch or coffee. We check in on each other personally, sharing our successes and failures in ministry and family in a safe environment of grace. It is also an environment where our ideas can be bounced around and suggestions for life and ministry can be made openly and honestly.

The second thing to do so that you do not remain on your island is utilize resources provided by either your sending church and/or your sending agency. I have learned that the majority of the time our church planting partners are craving to pour into their church planter in the form of relationship building, conferences, encouraging phone calls, and personal development programs. Each one is an opportunity to allow your team to pour into you and your mission.

Everything about today's American culture seems to apply more honor and more prestige to a man rather than to a team. Living in Florida it has been fun to watch the progression of SpaceX. SpaceX is doing so many innovative and fun things regarding space exploration and engineering. I love how they reuse each rocket booster, landing it safely on the earth or on a drone ship somewhere in the Atlantic. SpaceX was founded by a man named Elon Musk. The curious thing about Musk is that his name is everywhere in the media when they speak about SpaceX, yet when you go to their company website all you see is a few minor references or inspirational quotes from Musk. The company culture of team is what has gotten SpaceX to their current spot in the new race for space, not one man's personality

3. Tripp, *Dangerous Calling*, 84.

or skill set. If you are currently willing to sacrifice your emotional and relational health for the cult of your own individualized personality or success, you may want to step down or at least step away. Church planting is more fun when there is less stress. Less stress is found in teamwork. Team work is enabled by your partnerships. Run to your partnerships and stop sleeping on the floor.

The third and last difference maker that I have found to prevent island living is to enjoy life. Early on in ministry I felt this need to isolate myself for the purpose of workaholism. I didn't even know what that was, but I felt that I had to be the last one in the office, the one who used the least amount of vacation time and even the one who always had to check in when I actually went on a family vacation. I liked the island of my job and didn't want to enjoy fellowship off of my island.

But where does this come from? Why are we so content to sacrifice your eight-year-old's piano recital for the sake of a church plant team meeting? Maybe Kevin DeYoung put it best:

> I think most Christians hear these urgent calls to do more (or feel them internally already) and learn to live with a low-level guilt that comes from not doing enough. We know we can always pray more and give more and evangelize more, so we get used to living in a state of mild disappointment with ourselves.[4]

Ouch! I realize that he is speaking of Christians in general, but sadly, ministry leaders like you and I are setting a rather ridiculous example. I have learned that for long-term health I need to make time for friends. Contrary to what some old-timer ministry leaders may tell you, you can have friends in the church and you can also have friends who don't go to your church. I love shooting guns and fishing with other guys and I love double-dating with other couples. I treasure going to college football games with my son and I will always have time to sit and sip a Frappuccino with my girls. I take vacations...all the time! God gave us a great big, beautiful world and I intend to see it with my wife. We refuse to wait and see it on television from our wheelchairs. Our attitudes have changed somewhat in this regard. We only have so many days with each other and with our children. I don't know when those days on earth will run out, but I know that the first time my daughter walked into Disney World while holding my hand is an experience that I will never forget, and one that fuels me in so

4. DeYoung, *Crazy Busy*, 47.

many other areas of my life (like ministry). Enjoy life for it is one of God's many gifts to you. He will build his church.

Don't Chase Culture, Chase Jesus

It is probably appropriate to close with a discussion on overcoming one of the greatest potential unseen sources of frustration for you and me as church planters moving forward. I feel that we are too often trying to use shifting culture as our metric or our mark. We might not admit it out loud, but we feel it is part of our mission to slay the culture around us and bring everyone into our church. The problem is that of windmills.

In his classic work, *Don Quixote,* author Miguel de Cervantes, famously paints a picture of Don Quixote's great desire to gain honor as a knight by slaying the mighty giants. The problem is that the "giants" he is chasing are actually windmills. Every time he tries to attack the windmill "giants" they move and cause more problems. Much like culture today, when our target is culture, we are going to always be facing a moving target. Much like Quixote, we run the potential of causing confusion, frustration and hurt when we make our life and ministry about taming a subjective and increasingly elusive target.

Your life as a church planter is probably already full of statements piercing your heart. Statements that sound like, "Do this!" or "Be that!". You will never be at a loss for voices in your life of those who question you and say, "Have you considered?" Those conversations can be helpful when they come from the right person with the right heart, but don't allow the statement or demand of the day to dictate your success or failure in ministry.

It was 2006 when we left Florida to move back to my home in Pennsylvania. The purpose was to plant a church in a culture that I felt I could identify with. What I found was that I needed a season of re-education with regard to Pennsylvania culture because it was changing. Not as fast as some areas of the country, but it was changing. So, when we decided to move back to southwest Florida, I thought my cultural learning curve would be fairly flat, and I would slip on my Florida expertise like I slip on my nightly moccasin slippers. The problem was that as culture begins to change at an exponential rate, all the things that I think will work are already outdated.

Outdated in a church planting sense starts to look like throwing things against a wall to see what will stick. It is not a very productive method because it is not rooted in anything concrete. Through the ages it has been the truth of Christ and the commitment to it that has resulted in kingdom gains and sure footing. Jesus reminded his followers of this important fact in his analogy of building a house: "Everyone then who hears these words of mine and does them will be like a wise man who built his house on the rock. And the rain fell, and the floods came, and the winds blew and beat on that house, but it did not fall, because it had been founded on the rock." (Matt 7:24–25) You may not be building a physical house, but you are building a very real, spiritual house. Just like our discussion of donuts earlier, make sure that your ministry is rooted and built up on Christ's word and truth, rather than a shifting culture that will be forever finicky and forever disapproving.

Being a church planter and a church that stands for something rooted in Christ is probably going to make you feel different. It will probably tempt you to chuck the ball as far down field as you can. It may even cause some additional pain. However, the word doesn't change. The message is the same yesterday, today and forever, and because of that, I can sleep confidently knowing that I'm on the right path.

Stand Tall

We have spoken a lot in this book about work and metrics, firm expectations and hypotheticals so I feel it is important to share words of affirmation over you. Your work is hard, that's for sure. The work of church planting is small in scope at times and off the radar of many whom you will encounter. You are going to spend many days doubting your efforts and doubting that fruit will ever come. You are going to lament your decisions and you are going to lament your position. Yet here you are in the middle of an amazing journey.

I commend you and pray for you. Your days are not insignificant because God's work is never insignificant. Your work is not small because God is not small. You are most assuredly on God's radar even if others are passing by you. Your value is not in the size of your ministry, nor is it in the degree that you hold or the speed by which you grow. Your value rests in the work of Christ alone. You have been crucified with Christ. The life you live now as a church planter, a husband, a team member, a daddy or a partner, you now live by faith in the Son of God, who loved you and gave himself for you. (Gal 2:20) Your identity begins and ends at the cross of Jesus Christ. Your work begins and ends there too. May that work never feel ordinary, but rather, may you always know how extraordinary it truly is!

Bibliography

Akin, Daniel. *10 Who Changed the World*. Nashville: B&H, 2012.

Allender, Dan B. *Leading with a Limp: Take Full Advantage of Your Most Powerful Weakness*. Colorado Springs: Waterbrook, 2008.

Blanchard, Ken, Phil Hodges, and Phyllis Hendry. *Lead Like Jesus Revisited: Lessons from The Greatest Leadership Role Model of All Time*. Nashville: Nelson, 2016.

Christopherson, Jeff. "Can We Now Agree that It's Time to Become a Different Kind of Church?" https://www.christianitytoday.com/edstetzer/2020/july/can-we-now-agree-that-its-time-to-become-different-kind-of-.html.

———. *Kingdom Matrix: Designing a Church for the Kingdom of God*. Boise, ID: Russell Media, 2012.

Christopherson, Jeff and Mac Lake. *Kingdom First: Starting Churches That Shape Movements*. Nashville: Broadman & Holman, 2015.

DeYoung, Kevin. *Crazy Busy: A (Mercifully) Short Book About a (Really) Big Problem*. Wheaton, IL: Crossway, 2013.

Hunt, Johnny M. *Building Your Leadership Resume*. Nashville: B&H, 2009.

Hunter III, George G. *The Celtic Way of Evangelism: How Christianity Can Reach the West...Again*. Nashville: Abingdon, 2000.

Idleman, Kyle. *Not a Fan*. Grand Rapids, MI: Zondervan, 2011.

MacArthur Jr., John. *The Body Dynamic: Finding Where You Fit in Today's Church*. Colorado Springs: Chariot Victor, 1996.

Majewski, Taylor. "A Brief History of Etsy On Its 10th Anniversary." https://www.builtinnyc.com/2015/11/04/brief-history-etsy.

Maxwell, John C. *The 21 Irrefutable Laws of Leadership: Follow Them and People Will Follow You*. Rev. and updated 10th ann. ed. Nashville: Thomas Nelson, 2007.

McIntosh, Gary. *Taking Your Church to the Next Level: What Got You Here Won't Get You There*. Grand Rapids: Baker, 2009.

Mohler, R. Albert. *We Cannot Be Silent*. Nashville: Nelson, 2015.

Rainer, Thom S. *I Am a Church Member*. Nashville: B&H, 2013.

Ryle, J.C. *Practical Religion*. Carlisle, PA: Banner & Truth Trust, 2013.

Sanders, J. Oswald. *Spiritual Leadership: Principles of Excellence for Every Believer*. Chicago: Moody, 1994.

Scazzero, Peter. *The Emotionally Healthy Leader: How Transforming Your Inner Life Will Deeply Transform Your Church, Team, and the World*. Grand Rapids: Zondervan, 2015.

Stetzer, Ed and Warren Bird. "The State of Church Planting in the United States: Research Overview and Qualitative Study of Primary Church Planting Entities." www.christianitytoday.com/assets/10228.pdf.

Sutton, Jerry. *A Matter of Conviction: A History of Southern Baptist Engagement with the Culture.* Nashville: B&H, 2008.

Tripp, Paul David. *Dangerous Calling: Confronting the Unique Challenges of Pastoral Ministry.* Wheaton, IL: Crossway, 2015.

Wesley, Charles. *Preface to Standard Sermons.* http://people.exeter.ac.uk/pellison/wesley/v1/prf.htm.

Whiteford, Scott. "The 'Bill Walsh Model' to Your Leadership Legacy." https://talentplus.com/the-bill-walsh-model-to-your-leadership-legacy.

Willis, Dustin and Aaron Coe. *Life On Mission: Joining the Everyday Mission of God.* Chicago: Moody, 2014.